Herman Maril
The Strong Forms of Our Experience

Herman Maril
The Strong Forms of Our Experience

Ann Prentice Wagner

UNIVERSITY OF MARYLAND ART GALLERY

The exhibition is organized by the University of Maryland Art Gallery, College Park, in association with the Arkansas Arts Center, Little Rock.

It is made possible by generous grants from the Herman Maril Foundation and the Muller Foundation.

The Maryland State Arts Council is also supporting the exhibition.

Exhibition dates:
University of Maryland Art Gallery
September 7–December 9, 2016

Arkansas Arts Center
January 27–April 16, 2017

Copyright © 2016 University of Maryland Art Gallery. All rights reserved. This book may not be reproduced, in whole or in part (beyond that copying permitted by Sections 107 and 108 of the U.S. Copyright Law, and except by reviewers from the public press), without written permission from the publisher.

Produced by the University of Maryland Art Gallery
2202 Parren J. Mitchell Art-Sociology Building
3834 Campus Drive
College Park, MD 20742
www.artgallery.umd.edu

Designed by JJ Chrystal
Edited by Lindsey Reinstrom

Photographed by Lee Stalsworth unless otherwise noted.

Typeset in Neue Hass Unica Pro and Meta Serif, and printed on Endurance Silk.
Printed and bound in Baltimore, Maryland, by Mount Royal Printing and Communications.
All images are in inches, centimeters, height x width.

Library of Congress
Cataloging-in-Publication Data:
Herman Maril: the strong forms of our experience/Ann Prentice Wagner.
pages cm
Includes bibliographical references and index.
ISBN 978-0-9961126-1-1 (softcover)
1. American artists—Exhibitions. I. Wagner, Ann, author. II. University of Maryland Art Gallery. III. Arkansas Arts Center.
2016952100

10 9 8 7 6 5 4 3 2 1

6	INTRODUCTION
10	ESSAY
51	CATALOGUE
146	EXHIBITION CHECKLIST
150	CHRONOLOGY
160	BIBLIOGRAPHY

INTRODUCTION

It is a privilege for me to be able to be author and curator of this important exhibition of Herman Maril's art mounted by the University of Maryland Art Gallery and hosted by the Arkansas Arts Center. The story of this exhibition and the accompanying catalog is a long one, featuring many people to whom I and the rest of the exhibition and publication team owe thanks. Although there have been many major exhibitions and publications of Herman Maril's works since the 1930s, this catalog is the longest narrative yet published about this important modern American artist. The research has been time-consuming and demanding. Thanks to the help of many, we have been able to correct errors and exclusions in previous publications to achieve a better understanding of Maril's life and career.

This project would have been impossible without the generous support of the Herman Maril Foundation, the Maryland State Arts Council, and the Muller Foundation. We are eternally grateful to them.

At the University of Maryland Art Gallery, the leadership of the team has passed from former Director John Shipman to current Director Taras W. Matla. Their commitment and creativity have been crucial to this exhibition and catalog. Many thanks to Lindsey Reinstrom for editing the catalog. We are also grateful to Madeline Gent, Graduate Assistant and Collections Registrar, and Abimbola Dawson, Business Manager. Others at the University of Maryland who have been important in this project are: Bonnie Thornton Dill, Dean, College of Arts and Humanities; Wendy Jacobs, Associate Dean and Equity Administrator; and Dorit Yaron, Deputy Director, David C. Driskell Center.

Many other people at the University of Maryland have been in my corner, including Henry "Quint" Gregory, of the Michelle Smith Collaboratory for Visual Culture and his now-retired colleague, Lauree J. Sails. This Maryland alumna is forever grateful to all of my fellow Terrapins.

Since my arrival at the Arkansas Arts Center in 2012 as Curator of Drawings, I have been delighted to find a warm welcome and great support for *Herman Maril: The Strong Forms of Our Experience*. In fact, Herman Maril was already a part of the collection before I came along. I am grateful to Executive Director Todd Herman, Chief Curator Brian J. Lang, Exhibition Designer Keith Melton, Curator for Exhibitions Matthew Smith, Curator for Collections Katie Hall Garner, Chief Preparator Alex Moomey, and Assistant Preparator Sam Jones. Further thanks go to Director of Development Kelly Fleming, Development Officer Beverly Kleckner, Director of Marketing and Communications Angel Galloway, Communications Manager Kelly Cargill Crow, Foundation Relations Manager Susannah Beachboard, Marketing Coordinator Daniella Napolitano, and Shop Manager Kim White.

My work on Herman Maril leading to this exhibition began in 2008 through the Smithsonian American Art Museum, when then Deputy Chief Curator George Gurney contacted me about researching and writing for the exhibition *1934: A New Deal for Artists*. Maril was one of the fifty-four artists in the exhibition. Many thanks to George Gurney for getting me involved. Thanks also to our mutual friend Wendy Wick Reaves, then Curator of Prints and Drawings at the National Portrait Gallery. I was writing entries for the National Portrait Gallery book and exhibition *Reflections/Refractions: Self-Portraiture in the Twentieth-Century*, when George reached out to me.

My research about Herman Maril for *1934: A New Deal for Artists* caught the attention of David Maril, Herman Maril's son and the director of the Herman Maril Foundation. David took me to the family home, the headquarters of the Herman

Fig. 1 *Herman Maril in his Baltimore Studio,* 1982, Herman Maril Foundation

Maril Foundation, in the lovely Mount Washington neighborhood of Baltimore. The house is filled with Maril's art, which immediately impressed and interested me. I enthusiastically accepted the offer to join the team. David has been a consistent help ever since, as I have gotten to know Herman Maril and his world. David has shown me art, shared stories and insights through many interviews, answered countless questions, cooked me lunches, put me up at the Maril home in Provincetown, lent and given me books, video recordings, and articles, introduced me to people who knew his father, trusted me to dig through the Maril family archival files, and generally done everything possible to make this a wonderful experience for the past eight years. And yet, David insists that he should give only information and access; the opinions expressed in the exhibition and publication are my own and independent. To David go my heartfelt thanks.

David introduced me to his cousin, Ronald Becker, a former Smithsonian Institution administrator who has played an important part in this project. Ron was very close with his uncle and helped me to feel closer to Herman Maril. David Maril also set up an interview with his sister, Nadja Maril Crilly. She and her family gave me a warm welcome into their house and told many great stories. While I was not able to meet Esta Maril before her passing, I feel almost as if I had met her, due to visiting her home, reading her letters and publications, and rifling through her files. I hope she would be pleased with my work. Many thanks to the whole family.

I am deeply grateful to the friends and colleagues of Herman Maril to whom David introduced me and who kindly consented to be interviewed for this project. They are: Irvin Greif, Richard Klank, Bill and Louise Rowles, and Mark Sherwin. Others with whom I have visited and from whom I have received encouragement include Christine M. McCarthy, Executive Director and Exhibition Curator of the Provincetown Art Association and Museum, as well as Lee Findlay Potter, Louis Newman, Janay Wong, and Dallas Dunn

Throughout the process of research, I have turned to the staff of the Smithsonian American Art Museum and National Portrait Gallery Library, including Anne Evenhaugen and her past colleagues, Doug Litts, Stephanie Moye, Alice Clarke, and Cecilia Chin. The staff of the Archives of American Art, including Marissa Bourgoin, Head of Reference, have also been invaluable to my work, as for so many researchers in the field.

I have also received vital aid from Karen Schneider of the Phillips Collection Library and Archives, Emily Rafferty of the Baltimore Museum of Art Archives, and Maria Day, Director of Special Collections at the Maryland State Archives.

Special thanks to those loaning art works to the exhibition: The Herman Maril Foundation, David Maril, Nadja Maril Crilly, Justin Patrick, and the University of Maryland.

The safe travel of the art is thanks to Bonsai Fine Arts. Thanks go to Lap Tran, CEO and Special Projects Supervisor, Scott Pittman, President and CFO, and their careful staff.

I am grateful for the lasting moral support of family and friends. I regret that my mother, Polly S. Wagner, did not live to see this exhibition and catalog about which she had heard so much. But I look forward to sharing them with my aunt Sue and uncle Bill Grice and with encouraging friends Elizabeth MacKenzie Tobey, Leslie Brice, Beila S. Organic, Miriam Cole Organic, and Ann Potter.

On behalf of the whole exhibition and publication team, thank you, everyone! I hope you are happy with the exhibition and the catalog. Herman Maril's great art deserves only the best.

ANN PRENTICE WAGNER, PHD

HERMAN MARIL: THE STRONG FORMS OF OUR EXPERIENCE

CHAPTER ONE

We know Herman Maril through his paintings, drawings, and prints—spare but evocative modernist images of the Maryland countryside, street corners in his home city of Baltimore, his family's homes, and the Cape Cod shores where he spent his summers. Maril was best known for his oil paintings, but this exhibition focuses on the large and important body of art he created on paper throughout his career. The drawings, watercolors, acrylic paintings on paper, and prints featured in this exhibition came into being in the context of the artist's oil paintings.

Maril believed in simplification in his art—making what he called "a stark statement."[1] His images, whether on paper or canvas, give us few descriptive details. However, each aspect of color, light, touch, and composition communicates the man. He shows us what he loves. First there is art itself. These are paintings and drawings that are plainly about painting and drawing. Maril loved these creative experiences. "I started painting the day I was born," the artist said.[2] This poetic exaggeration communicates Maril's complete and passionate identification as an artist from his earliest days. He told an interviewer, "I was always interested in painting. I cannot remember any period in my life in which I was not interested in painting."[3]

However, Maril never allowed the practical considerations of his creative life to override his devotion to family and home. When the pursuit of his art career might have recommended a move to the center of the American art world in New York City, this artist chose to remain in his native Baltimore. Yet Maryland was not his only home; Maril created a second home in Provincetown, Massachusetts, the famous artists' colony. In both locations, he kept his family and friends close at hand, but he also actively reached out to the wider world.

Maril wrote of his home city, "I find that I can work here and truly concentrate…. One can do one's work here and not feel isolated. Living in Baltimore offers a type of serenity to me, and at the same time it is not too far away from a few other places. When I want to see the galleries and museums in New York City, or have contact with some of my out-of-town artist friends, I can hop on a train and be there in a couple of hours."[4] He traveled to pursue his career and to explore the visual world, spending time in Washington, D.C., Philadelphia, New York, and many other places farther afield in the United States and abroad. Maril exhibited his art often in galleries and museums in New York, as well as in venues all around the United States and the world. Yet Baltimore remained the center of his life.

Words like poetic and lyrical come easily to mind when contemplating Herman Maril's paintings, drawings, and prints.[5] His individualistic style of modernism communicates the deep joy he found in familiar landscapes, seascapes, home interiors, and beloved people and animals. However, art-making was not an easy or carefree process for Maril, nor was the life of an artist undemanding. He had a strong work ethic. He saw no use in being a temperamental artist. He went to work early and labored for long hours in the studio, like a good worker in any field. Maril said, "I don't wait for inspiration. I believe inspiration comes with perspiration."[6] Becoming an artist in the first place was not easy for him. His art career was born of struggle. It took years for him to establish the approach through which he created images of such strength and beauty. Examining the artist's life affords insights into both Herman Maril's poetic art and the prosaic process through which he created it.

Herman Maril, originally named Hyman Becker, was born on October 13, 1908. Herman, who was never called by his legal name of Hyman, was the youngest of six children of a women's clothing worker named Isaac H. Becker and his wife, the former Celia Maril. The other children were Mazie, Morris, Rose, Joseph, and Deborah. Both parents had been born in Lithuania in about 1879. The artist's father worked in Baltimore's thriving garment industry as a cutter and at times a tailor, who also designed clothing.[7] Herman later took his mother's maiden name of Maril as his own last name and at that time also officially changed his first name to Herman.[8]

The artist diplomatically described his origins as "rather low income."[9] Maril's parents were far from well off, although they did better financially than many of the poverty-stricken Jewish families employed doing manual work in the textile mills.[10] Financial considerations were an overriding practical concern, so the dream of being an artist was a difficult one for young Herman. It required courage and devotion for him to see it through. But where did this art vision come from? The setting of Maril's youth hardly seemed a likely background for a great artist, although his father did creative work as a clothing designer. Herman recalled, "'There weren't any artists in the family. I just picked it up.'"[11]

The Becker family lived at 3810 Park Heights Avenue, in the northwest area of Baltimore, near the city's many textile mills. Their neighborhood was populated by Isaac Becker's fellow textile workers, many of them also Jewish.[12] Herman Maril's son David grew up hearing about Herman Maril's childhood spent in the Beckers' straight-laced, even oppressive Orthodox Jewish home. Maril wrote in his journal, "Open spacious areas in my childhood must have presented a pleasant contrast to some unpleasant and highly limited situations."[13] Having an artist in the family was a foreign concept that roused hostility from some family members. While the aspiring artist's parents allowed their youngest son to continue to live under their roof as he worked toward his goal, painting was not the type of career that they would have had in mind for him. Maril said, "'My parents were poor, and they didn't encourage me or discourage me. If that's what I wanted to do, it was all right with them.'"[14] Isaac Becker was more encouraging to his son's artistic aspirations than was his wife.[15] Another very supportive member of the family was Herman's sister, Mazie Becker, who was nine years older than the artist. Mazie became a social worker; understanding toward others was among her leading characteristics. With the moral support of Mazie and their father, Herman braved the skepticism of other family members.[16] His interest in art arose early and eventually this love carried all before it.

Unfortunately, none of Maril's juvenile art works survive, so the only way to see his early creative efforts is through the lens of stories reported and recalled after his standing as an artist was established. Maril is said to have made his own toys rather than merely accepting the playthings presented to him.[17] But his most significant early creations were drawings. Stories about the artist begin with Maril's drawing even before he could talk.[18] Among the drawings mentioned in stories was a Baltimore trolley Herman drew on a blackboard when he was in second grade. During World War I, in about 1916 or 1917, the boy startled teachers with a perfectly recognizable portrait he had drawn of Kaiser Wilhelm. This image was presumably inspired by a newspaper photograph. The teacher's reaction to this portrait of the reviled leader of the enemy nation was to invite all of the young pupils to walk by and defile it. Young Herman was already learning about the strange power of images.[19] The mental picture of proud parents and teachers praising the child helps to illuminate the beginnings of Maril's self-identification as an artist in spite of his working class origins. Maril recalled, "When I was a kid my whole involvement, besides being a kid, was the arts someway."[20]

Art as it was taught at Maril's elementary school, Public School No. 40, at Asquith and Orleans Streets, did not appeal to the boy. The adult artist said disdainfully, "'They made you draw a tree the way the teacher said.'"[21] Naturally, a modernist looking back would take pride in the early evidence of his creative independence; he wanted to draw a tree or anything else just the way he conceived it.

Maril recalled another school art experience as crucial to his development. What would later become the Walters Art Gallery, the private collection of William Walters, was opened to Baltimore public school children each year. The young Maril was powerfully moved by his first in-person views of old master and nineteenth-century works. These were perhaps his earliest models for what art really was, since his humble childhood home would scarcely have had original paintings on the walls. "That was a great thrill," Maril recalled of visiting the Walters collection.[22] "'That turned out to be a very exciting experience for me. It was amazing to come into contact with so many beautiful works of art when I was young.'"[23] Early Italian Renaissance paintings were some of his favorites. He must have thought about the people who had made these wondrous creations and what it would be like to be an artist. Looking back on the origins of his dream of being an artist, he said, "'I can remember even in the early grades in public school having some interest in painting.'"[24]

Herman Maril later said of his childhood, "I found that my greatest pleasures were looking at pictures and taking walks, and drawing."[25] From the beginning, he loved Baltimore. He nostalgically recalled "walks in my early childhood, with my father, exploring the wharves and looking at the many ships along the inner harbor. In my early youth I remember the many days I spent sketching from Federal Hill. This is a colorful city."[26] The mills and sweatshops in his own immediate neighborhood were hardly beautiful, but nearby Druid Hill Park provided a plethora of subjects for the young artist to draw. The park was the site of the Howard Peters Rawlings Conservatory and the Baltimore Zoo, where the boy could see plants and animals from all over the world. In the park Maril later depicted an ancient Osage orange tree that he had known all his life (cats. 13, 14).[27]

In nearby Washington, D.C., the young artist found a wider array of art institutions than were available in Baltimore. An artistic connection to America's capital city would be important to Maril throughout his creative life. Among his favorite Washington venues during his early years was the Corcoran Gallery, featuring both European and American works. He also visited the Smithsonian Institution, where the Freer Gallery of Art that was then the only art museum with its own building. Maril remembered, "I did very little copying, but was always interested in going to the museums."[28]

The collection assembled by Detroit businessman and art collector Charles Lang Freer opened as part of the Smithsonian Institution in Washington, D.C., in 1923, when Maril was fifteen years old.[29] In addition to its famous collection of Asian art, this handsome new museum included American late-nineteenth and early-twentieth-century art by artists such as James McNeill Whistler and Abbott Thayer.

Although Maril spoke little about Asian art or Whistler in recorded conservations or interviews, his early visits to the Freer may have helped to contribute to the Asian-influenced wash drawings he made decades later. During World War II, the soldier-artist advised fellow soldiers visiting Washington, D.C., to include the Freer on their itinerary.[30]

Young Herman loved to visit the Phillips Memorial Gallery, later to be the Phillips Collection, which opened in the home of Duncan Phillips in Washington, D.C., in 1921.[31] He reminisced, "Well, I had the greatest access to the Phillips Gallery in Washington, D.C. which was a small, homey museum where you could sit and look at the pictures and talk to someone, enjoy it, and really spend a lot of time. I really got a great deal from the Phillips Gallery in Washington—as a matter of fact my first experiences [sic] in seeing actual art was at the Phillips Gallery ... other than in books."[32] Maril here discounted those early visits to the Walters collection and other Washington museums he could have seen before 1921; his emphasis shows his focus on the modern art he saw at the Phillips Memorial Gallery.

Maril attended high school at Baltimore Polytechnic Institute, a highly respected technical school that had been founded in 1883. Its strong reputation allowed students who did well there to expect that they might advance to the finest engineering colleges in the country.[33] His artistic ambitions were momentarily displaced by the idea of being a civil engineer. Maril recalled his dreamy "'romantic reasons.... What appealed to me was the idea of building bridges everywhere.'"[34] Judging from his mature art works, this interest in structure persisted all of Maril's life. One of his favorite subjects was a building under construction or burning down (cats. 5, 22, 50, 60, 72).

But engineering did not displace Maril's passion for art. A newspaper article told how his "first oil painting got him through an otherwise impassable chemistry course at Poly. He did the portrait of his chemistry professor; the old gentleman liked it so well he hung it in his classroom and, as Maril explains, it 'kinda made things easy for me.'" Maril was also art editor of the school newspaper the *Poly Press*.[35] Soon, any possibility of Maril's ever actually becoming an engineer faded as he made a decisive turn in the direction of art. He stated in 1947, "'I just found out I didn't have the mental equipment for a civil engineer.'"[36]

Maril was fortunate to be coming of age in a town with a serious art school. During his years at Poly, at night he attended classes at the Maryland Institute College of Art. He began these classes at about the age of fourteen.[37] The artist remembered, "At first, while I was going to high school, I enrolled at the night school. I lied about my age in order to get in."[38] The budding artist's father had enough belief in his son's potential to help him get into the school.[39] As is traditional for academic art education, his lessons for the first two years focused on drawing in charcoal from plaster casts of classical sculptures. Then there were two years of drawing the figure from life.[40] Maril professed to hate the dry work copying someone else's art rather than making his own images from life, but he was determined to stick with it so he could become an artist.[41] Working from live models must have been more stimulating for the young man. His school friends were shocked to learn that he was painting from nude models.[42]

During his high school years, Maril used his talents to bring in money from commercial artwork. He learned from a sign painter how to letter show cards advertising local stores. He gradually stepped up his skills and his level of pay. He continued this kind of work until at least the 1940s.[43] Examples of Maril's lettering projects are preserved in the Maril Foundation collection because he sometimes made watercolors on the backs of failed signs.

The greatest mystery of Herman Maril's artistic career lies at its beginning. Why was the son of an impecunious orthodox Jewish family with no known art background so determined to be an artist? How did he manage to emerge not only as a professional artist, but as a sophisticated modern painter before his twentieth birthday? Other than the artist's own gifts, the answer seems to lie in a complex of people and events surrounding his training at the Maryland Institute and the art life of the city of Baltimore in the 1920s. It is often difficult to document Maril's individual part in events, but the modernist enthusiasm in the city clearly shaped his art and his life.

While Maril was taking night classes at the Maryland Institute during high school, the school was under the direction of Alon Bement. Bement had come to Baltimore in 1920 from Teachers College at Columbia University in New York City, where he had been a protégé of the influential art educator Arthur Wesley Dow.[44] Bement exposed students at the Maryland Institute to European and American modern art, much as he and Dow had done previously for such New York students as the young Georgia O'Keeffe, who went on to become a great modernist painter.[45]

In Baltimore, Bement began a lively round of exhibitions and lectures to widen the horizons of the Institute's students. These exhibitions included, in 1923, a show of art by French modernist Henri Matisse in the collection assembled by Baltimore residents Dr. Claribel Cone and her younger sister Etta Cone.[46] We can presume that young Herman Maril saw the exhibition.

The Cohn sisters' collection of art by such giants of European modernism as Matisse, Paul Cézanne, and Pablo Picasso was a formative influence on Maril's modernist aesthetic.[47] The artist stated, "'The friendship of Etta Cone which allowed me to be a frequent visitor to her apartment, where I was able to see the great Matisses and other works in her collection, was a valuable addition to my learning.'"[48] Since Maril does not mention Dr. Claribel Cone, one may assume that his personal friendship with Etta Cone began after her older sister's death in 1929.

Maril knew the contents of the Baltimore sisters' adjoining apartments at the Marlborough well before the modernist masterpieces went to the Baltimore Museum of Art in 1950.[49] Maril's papers include letters to the artist from Etta Cone written in 1942 and 1948. The Cone sisters' papers at the Baltimore Museum of Art include a 1941 letter from Maril to Etta Cone in which Maril mentions visiting Miss Cone at home.[50] The warmth of the friendship already in place is clear, implying that Maril and Miss Cone had known each other for some time. The greatest part of the Cone sisters' collection was devoted to works by Henri Matisse. His familiarity with this outstanding collection helped Maril to identify with Matisse, whose work was a touchstone for him throughout his career. He said he saw ladies in art classes using twenty or more colors on their palettes, but creating work that was "dead." Maril said he "read about Matisse, who used six or seven colors on his palette and I observed the richness" of his paintings. The mature Maril would use a reductive palette inspired by the French modernist master.[51]

Most likely, Maril was introduced to Etta Cone by one of his teachers at the Maryland Institute, but not Henry Adams Roben, whom Maril recalled as being personally liberal but artistically conservative.[52] When he was studying under Roben and his colleagues, Maril made one of his earliest surviving works (fig. 2). This is a still life painting that Maril later habitually dismissed verbally as "student work."[53] The broadly brushed, dark image takes some elements of color and brushwork from the impressionist tradition as taught by William Merritt Chase. By then Chase's approach to painting was decidedly retrograde. But one can also see in this painting the beginning of a move toward a faceting of forms that recalls the work of Paul Cézanne.

Maril probably met Etta Cone through her friend Charles H. Walther, Baltimore's most innovative and influential modernist artist of the period. Walther had begun teaching at the Maryland Institute in 1906.[54] His art was remarkably cutting edge for American work of the time, particularly for an artist working outside of New York City. By the early 1910s, the Baltimore professor was working in a vein of abstraction clearly influenced by the nonrepresentational art of the German-based Russian artist Wassily Kandinsky (fig. 3). Maril recalled, "Of course, I was acquainted with [Wassily] Kandinsky's work through Charles Walther, who was a great admirer of Kandinsky."[55]

Walther was an important mentor for the younger artist.[56] Maril said, "He was one of the first really non-figurative painters, abstract painters, in this country … he and I, though I was somewhat of a rebel in his class, became very good friends. And we visited each other, since we lived close by, at least once a week. And though he was a much older man—I was in my late teens, actually—the relationship was a supportive thing … in my own searchings."[57] Walther lived on Pimlico Road, which intersected with Park Heights Avenue, where Maril and his parents lived. Maril's friend and teacher, like his young student, had been born in Baltimore and trained at the Maryland Institute. Walther, however, had the advantage of study at the Académie Julian in Paris and travels in Europe.[58]

After his graduation from high school in 1926, Maril began attending the Maryland Institute as a regular stu-

2. Herman Becker, *Still Life,* 1928, oil on canvas, 20 x 26 in. (50.8 x 66 cm), Herman Maril Foundation

3. Charles H. Walther, *Abstract #121,* 1915, oil on burlap, 13 x 16 in. (33 x 40.6 cm), Washington County Museum of Fine Arts, Hagerstown, Maryland

dent during the day. At night he did commercial art.[59] The beginning of Maril's serious art study was overshadowed by his mentor's conflicts with the Institute's new director. In 1925, Alon Bement left the Institute to become director of the Art Center in New York. Bement was replaced by the deeply conservative Hans Schuler.[60] Schuler, an academically trained sculptor most famous for his funeral monuments in Baltimore, completely banished modernism from classes and exhibitions at the institute.[61] For a few years Schuler allowed Walther to continue to teach at the Art Institute, but the situation was tense.

The friction between Walther and Schuler was due in part to an incident in December 1925. The Maryland Institute refused to exhibit the modernist art of young Baltimore painter Shelby Shackelford. When a modernist gallery was founded in Baltimore the following year, the *Baltimore Sun* noted, "The gallery, he [Charles H. Walther] said, was the inspiration of Miss Shelby Shackelford, a modernist painter, who was refused permission to exhibit her work at the Maryland Institute by Hans Schuler because he feared it might have a bad effect on the students."[62] Of course, Maril was one of those students over whom the director watched so closely.

Schuler communicated his antipathy to modern art in a statement to the press on the occasion of a local modern art exhibition that included work by Walther. Schuler said, "'Neither the officials of the institute nor I have any objection to a faculty member exhibiting modernist painting … provided that while teaching he observes the rules of the school…. At the institute Mr. Walther teaches perspective and the other fundamentals of art that are required by our rules. He does not inject his modernism into its class work. What he does outside the school is none of our business…. What the school does forbid and will continue to forbid is the exhibition within its walls of modernistic art and the teaching of modernism to students who are not yet ready to receive it.'"[63] For a Maryland Institute student like Maril, the sudden transformation of policies under Schuler after the modernist Bement made for stark changes.

The modernist exhibition about which Schuler spoke was mounted by a new Baltimore art organization known as "the Modernists."[64] They had come together at Shelby Shackelford's urging in December 1925, after the Art Institute's refusal of her exhibition, to establish modern art exhibition opportunities in Baltimore. They also brought information about modernism to the Baltimore public. There is no evidence that Herman Maril was an active part of the organization. However, the student must have been well aware of the Modernists and probably attended their exhibitions. The president of the organization was George Boas, an associate professor of philosophy at Johns Hopkins University.[65] Boas, an authority on aesthetics and art criticism as well as the history of philosophy, was an important figure in Baltimore's cultural life and a good friend of Claribel and Etta Cone.[66] Boas gave lectures to educate the Baltimore art public about modern art.[67] We do not know if Maril attended these lectures, but they surely would have interested him.

Walther installed the Modernists' first exhibition on January 16, 1926. The artists exhibited included Walther himself, Shelby Shackelford, Simone Brangier [George Boas' wife], John Graham, Lee Gatch, and Walter Bohanan. Gatch and Bohanan would exhibit alongside Maril in Baltimore for many years to come. John Graham became a modern artist and theorist of national importance, who gave advice about collecting modern art to both the Cone sisters and Duncan Phillips, the founder of the Phillips Collection.[68] A *Baltimore Sun* article about the Modernist exhibition quoted a young woman artist as saying, "'There'll be no influences of the Maryland Institute here…. Here's where our art will be given a chance with no one interfering.'"[69] Perhaps Maril was there as well, with similar thoughts in his mind. Certainly, his art was allied with Walther's modernism.

The word "Modernist" became a red flag waved more and more often by the Baltimore art press and art institutions. For instance, in 1926, the Baltimore Museum of Art declared that it would, for the first time, include modernist paintings and sculpture as a distinct division within its annual all-Baltimore exhibition. Charles Walther was the one-man jury for the modern works.[70] A *Sun* critic gave a jaded description of the exhibition and of the largely conservative Baltimore art world Maril was entering:

One finds that the dominant style is a modified impressionism influenced by the work of such men as [Leon] Kroll or [Jonas] Lie, by the Paris of '05. There are any number of portraits, there is a great and disconcerting weakness in the pictures in water colors, the sculpture too frequently runs to the old and outworn forms and symbolisms, the etchings are workmanlike rather than inspired. And against all of these things there is a section devoted to "modernism" to the inevitable "left" group, the aesthetic wild persons who even as modernists seem to have grown slightly old and tired.[71]

The modernist art was clearly the most vital work in the exhibition, even if it was not up to the critic's standards. But there was enough modernist work to interest and encourage an emerging artist like Maril. Indeed, the *Baltimore Sun* art critic signing himself "H. Kingston Fleming" stated that easily the best work in the exhibition was *Fantasia* by modernist Shelby Shackelford.[72] Modernism was making rapid gains at the just the moment when Maril was maturing. Every artist active in the city would have to decide whether he or she would side with tradition or with modernism. The young Herman Maril was attending classes ruled by the anti-modernist dictates of Schuler, but outside of school his great influences included the modernist Walther and the exhibitions at the Phillips Collection and the Modernists' exhibitions in Baltimore. There was intense pressure on the maturing Maril to align himself one way or the other.

In 1927, Baltimore hosted a pair of events that showed Maril and other Baltimoreans important American and modern art. In April, 1927, the Phillips Memorial Gallery in Washington, D.C., sent two exhibitions to Baltimore: *American Themes by American Painters*, to be shown at the Friends of Art, and *An Exhibition of Expressionist Painters from the Experiment Station of the Phillips Memorial Gallery*, at the Baltimore Museum of Art.[73] The Phillips Memorial Gallery exhibitions in Baltimore were highly praised by H. Kingston Fleming, the modernist-favoring *Baltimore Sun* critic, as "Probably the most important art exhibition[s] shown in Baltimore this season, or for that matter, the last two seasons."[74] Herman Maril must have taken notice of this attention, although he had already visited the Phillips Memorial Gallery for himself. The Phillips Collection began to collect Walther's works in 1927 as part of its support of regional artists.[75] Herman Maril often travelled the forty-five miles from Baltimore to Washington to keep up with what was on the walls in the Dupont Circle museum. He regularly visited the Phillips Collection for the rest of his life.[76]

In 1929, Herman Maril Becker began to sign his artwork with the name "Herman Maril."[77] He took his mother's maiden name to avoid confusion with another artist named Herman Becker.[78] The rival Herman Becker may have been Herman Albert Becker, a sculptor who was a year younger than the man who became Herman Maril.[79] The change of name signals the young artist's commitment to art. For the moment, Maril continued to legally be Hyman Becker; the name change became legal in September 1940.[80]

Maril's firm choice to go in a modernist direction shows in his self-portrait dated 1927–1929 and signed in bold block letters "Herman Maril" (fig. 4). The brushy impressionist-influenced aspects of the style of Maril's earlier still life is gone except for some dark areas of the background, apparently left over from when he began the painting in 1927. The crisp, geometric planes and warm colors of the figure and the landscape behind him show the influence of Paul Cézanne. What clearer indication of modernism's importance could Maril give than to model his self-portrait on the many self-portraits by the French modernist pioneer? Maril stated, "Cézanne was an important figure to me, a giant to me."[81]

Maril could easily have gotten to know Cézanne's work through reproductions, no doubt. But he also studied Cézanne's work in person in the Cone sisters' collection and the Phillips Collection.[82] More works by Cézanne were visible in New York. By the late 1920s, the French master was well known among American adherents of modern art.[83] Maril recalled that as a young man he avidly devoured Roger Fry's 1927 book, *Cézanne: A Study of His Development*.[84]

Maril felt that, "in reading Roger Fry, and learning about [Paul Cézanne], and … and going to see pictures, I think I had the advantage of being a little ahead of my contemporaries in that area."[85] This was a crucial period during which Maril learned lessons that would last him a lifetime. He asserted, "'I became aware of the abstract basis of all good painting in the late '20s particularly through seeing the works of

Cézanne and the post war French painters. I began to "feel" the inherent rightness of all works of art in their basic abstract concept.'"[86]

It was a surprisingly sophisticated Herman Maril who graduated from the Maryland Institute in 1928. The creative and financial challenges that lay before him were aptly symbolized by his failure to receive his diploma at his formal graduation because he owed a small amount of money to the school for his tuition.[87] This angered the young artist, who would never teach at the school where he had been trained. President Schuler's animosity toward modernism probably also contributed to the rebelliousness of the new graduate. Herman Maril remained in Baltimore, but he left behind the constraints of the conservative Maryland Institute. His sights were trained on the wider world.

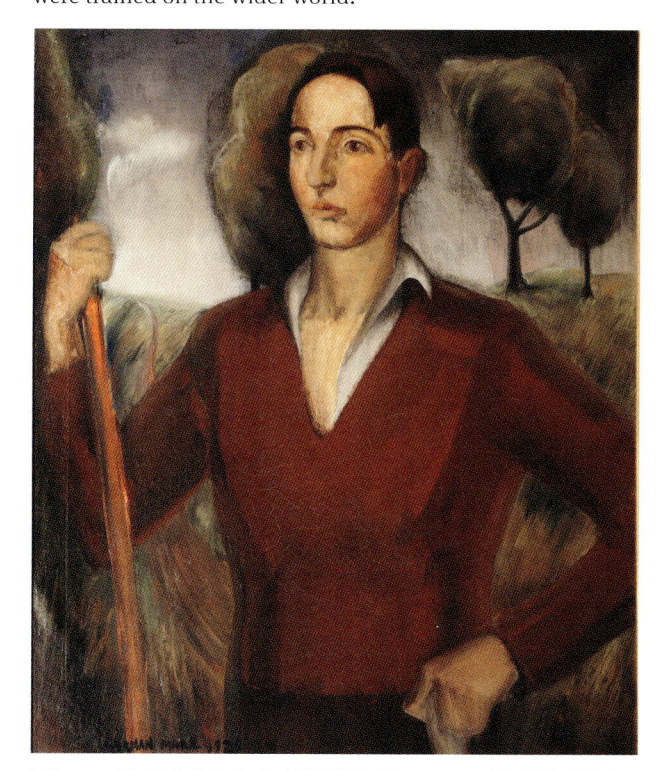

4. Herman Maril, *Self-Portrait,* 1927-1929, oil on canvas, 36 x 30 in. (91.4 x 76.2 cm), Collection of David Maril

Notes

1. *Herman Maril* (Baltimore, Maryland: Axis Video, 1981).

2. Herman Maril, interview by Ronald Becker, July 22, 1981, transcript, Archives of American Art, Herman Maril Foundation.

3. Herman Maril, interview by Dorothy Seckler, July 5, 1965, Archives of American Art, http://www.aaa.si.edu/collections/interviews/oral-history-interview-herman-maril-11701.

4. Herman Maril, "A Green and Quiet Place to Live….," *Baltimore Sun*, July 3, 1977, sec. K.

5. John Dorsey, "Herman Maril: Baltimore Artist Captured Both the Linear and the Lyric," *Baltimore Sun*, September 9, 1986, sec. C.

6. Audrey Bishop, "At Home with Herman Maril, Unofficial Dean of Maryland Painters," *News American*, October 12, 1980, sec. C.

7. "1930 United States Federal Census," 1930.

8. Frank Getlein, *Herman Maril* (Baltimore, MD: Baltimore Museum of Art, 1967), 10.; Beverly Oppenheimer, "Ex Parte in the Matter of the Petition of Hyman Becker for Change of Name" (Circuit Court of Baltimore City, September 25, 1940), Maryland State Archives, Annapolis, Maryland. The legal papers for Maril's change of name state that while the artist's legal name was given on his birth certificate as Hyman Becker; he always used the first name Herman.

9. Herman Maril, interview by Dorothy Seckler, July 5, 1965.

10. Jo Ann E. Argersinger, "The City That Tries to Suit Everybody: Baltimore's Clothing Industry," *Baltimore Book: New Views of Local History* (Philadelphia: Temple University Press, 1991), 80–101.

11. VIsaac Rehert, "The Need to Give Oneself More Time," *Baltimore Sun*, February 28, 1977, sec. B, 1.

12. Argersinger, "The City That Tries to Suit Everybody: Baltimore's Clothing Industry," 81–83.; Bill Harvey, "Hampden-Woodberry: Baltimore's Mill Villages," *The Baltimore Book: New Views of Local History* (Philadelphia: Temple University Press, 1991), 38–55.

13. Herman Maril, "Herman Maril Journal," 1971, 1983, Herman Maril Foundation.

14. Rehert, "The Need to Give Oneself More Time," 1.

15. David Maril, "Re: Genealogy Research," email, October 4, 2015.

16. David Maril, interview by Ann Prentice Wagner, March 15, 2010.

17. Emery Grossman, *Art and Tradition* (New York: T. Yoseloff, 1968), 101.

18. Bishop, "At Home with Herman Maril, Unofficial Dean of Maryland Painters."

19 Alfred D. Charles, "From Show Card Writing to Metropolitan Museum," *Baltimore Sun*, November 3, 1940, sec. M.

20 Herman Maril, interview by Ronald Becker.

21 Charles, "From Show Card Writing to Metropolitan Museum."

22 Herman Maril, interview by Dorothy Seckler.

23 William Hauptman, *Herman Maril* (College Park, MD: University of Maryland Art Department Gallery, 1977), 17.

24 Ibid.

25 Herman Maril, interview by Dorothy Seckler.

26 Maril, "A Green and Quiet Place to Live…."

27 Tim Wheeler, "Storm Claims Baltimore's Oldest, Largest Tree," *Baltimore Sun*, October 31, 2012, http://articles.baltimoresun.com/2012-10-31/features/bal-bmg-storm-claims-one-of-baltimores-oldest-largest-trees-20121031_1_tree-species-druid-hill-park-city-forestry-workers.

28 Herman Maril, interview by Dorothy Seckler.

29 Thomas Lawton, *Freer: A Legacy of Art* (Washington, D.C.: New York: Freer Gallery of Art, Smithsonian Institution, in association with H. N. Abrams, 1993), 252.

30 Herman Maril, "Places of Interest Free to Servicemen in Washington" (Baker's Batter, May 1, 1944), Herman Maril Foundation.

31 Phillips Collection and Eliza E. Rathbone, *Duncan Phillips Centennial Exhibition* (Washington, D.C.: Phillips Collection, 1999), 6.

32 Herman Maril, interview by Ronald Becker.

33 Baltimore Polytechnic Institute, "Web Site Baltimore Polytechnic Institute," Baltimore Polytechnic Institute web site, accessed February 15, 2015, http://www.bpi.edu/history.jsp/.; David Maril, "Baltimore Polytechnic Institute," email, February 15, 2015.

34 Bishop, "At Home with Herman Maril, Unofficial Dean of Maryland Painters."

35 Charles, "From Show Card Writing to Metropolitan Museum."

36 "Artist Once Hoped to Become Engineer," *Baltimore Evening Sun*, October 24, 1947.

37 Bishop, "At Home with Herman Maril, Unofficial Dean of Maryland Painters."

38 Herman Maril, interview by Dorothy Seckler.

39 Elsa A. Solender, "Baltimore Painter Herman Maril: Silent Serenity and Complex Logic," *Baltimore Jewish Times*, March 15, 1985, 60.

40 Hauptman, *Herman Maril*, 17, 20.

41 Charles, "From Show Card Writing to Metropolitan Museum."

42 Elsa A. Solender, "Baltimore Painter Herman Maril: Silent Serenity and Complex Logic," 60.

43 Herman Maril, intrview by Ronald Becker.; Charles, "From Show Card Writing to Metropolitan Museum."

44 "Maryland Institute Head Is Named by Governors," *Baltimore Sun*, July 14, 1920.; Douglas L. Frost and College of Art, Maryland Institute, *MICA: Making History, Making Art* (Baltimore, MD: Maryland Institute College of Art, 2010), 133–35.

45 Roxana Robinson, *Georgia O'Keeffe: A Life* (Hanover and London: University Press of New England, 1989), 80–81.

46 Frost and Maryland Institute, *MICA*, 133–137.

4 Ellen B. Hirschland and Nancy H. Ramage, *The Cone Sisters of Baltimore: Collecting at Full Tilt* (Evanston, IL: Northwestern University Press, 2008).; Jack Flam et al., *Matisse in the Cone Collection: The Poetics of Vision; Publ. on the Occasion of the Reopening of the Cone Collection, April 22, 2001* (Baltimore, MD: Baltimore Museum of Art, 2001).; Brenda Richardson, William C. Ameringer, and Baltimore Museum of Art., *Dr. Claribel & Miss Etta: The Cone Collection of the Baltimore Museum of Art* (Baltimore, MD: Baltimore Museum of Art, 1985).

48 Hauptman, *Herman Maril*, 24.

49 Richardson, Ameringer, et al., *Dr. Claribel & Miss Etta*, 9.

50 Etta Cone, "Letter from Etta Cone to Herman Maril," letter, (January 20, 1942), Herman Maril Foundation.; Etta Cone, "Letter from Etta Cone to Herman Maril," letter, (June 11, 1948), Herman Maril Foundation.; Herman Maril, "Letter from Herman Maril to Etta Cone about the Exhibition of Her Collection at the Baltimore Museum," letter, (June 7, 1941), Baltimore Museum of Art Archives, Cone Sisters Papers.

51 *Herman Maril* (Baltimore, Maryland: Axis Video, 1981).

52 Herman Maril, interview by Dorothy Seckler.

53 David Maril, interview by Ann Prentice Wagner.

54 Frost and Maryland Institute, *MICA*, 137.

55 Herman Maril, interview by Dorothy Seckler.

56 Herman Maril, interview by Robert Brown, July 21, 1971, Archives of American Art.

57 Herman Maril, interview by Dorothy Seckler.

58 "C. H. Walther, Noted Artist, Dies of Injury," *Baltimore Sun*, May 8, 1938.

59 Charles, "From Show Card Writing to Metropolitan Museum."

60 Frost and Maryland Institute, *MICA*, 137.

61 Fred Rasmussen, "Monumental City's Monument Maker Sculptor: Hans Schuler Left His Mark on the Maryland Institute, College of Art and in Many Public Places around His Hometown," *Baltimore Sun*, October 19, 1997.

62 "Maryland Institute Instructor Exhibits at Modernist Gallery," *Baltimore Sun*, January 16, 1926.

63 "Will Not Oppose Instructor's Exhibiting of Modernist Work," *Baltimore Sun*, January 17, 1926.

64 Frost and Maryland Institute, *MICA*, 137.

65 "Advises Modernist Art Group Disband," *Baltimore Sun*, October 24, 1926.

66 Alicia G. Longwell, "John Graham and the Quest for an American Art in the 1920s and 1930s" (City University of New York, 2007), 55.; Philip P. Wiener, "In Memoriam: George Boas (1891-1980)," *Journal of the History of Ideas* 41, no. 3 (September 1980): 453.

67 "Will Discuss Modernism," *Baltimore Sun*, January 21, 1926.

68 University of Maryland, College Park, *350 Years of Art & Architecture in Maryland*, eds. Mary A. Dean and Arthur R. Blumenthal (College Park, MD: University of Maryland Art Gallery and University of Maryland Gallery of the School of Architecture, 1984), 99, 101.

69 "Maryland Institute Instructor Exhibits at Modernist Gallery."

70 "Museum Will Show Baltimore Modernist Art for First Time," *Baltimore Sun*, March 17, 1926.

71 A. D. E., "Further Views on All-City Show at Baltimore Museum," *Baltimore Sun*, April 11, 1926.

72 H. K. F., "Shackelford Canvas Said to Take Honors in All-City Show," *Baltimore Sun*, March 28, 1926, sec. MT.

73 Duncan Phillips, *An Exhibition of Expressionist Painters from the Experiment Station of the Phillips Memorial Gallery* (Washington, D.C.: Phillips Memorial Gallery, 1927).; Duncan Phillips, *Catalogue of the Exhibition of American Themes by American Painters Lent by Phillips Memorial Gallery, Washington, D.C.* (Washington, D.C.: Phillips Memorial Gallery, 1927).; Duncan Phillips, Erika D. Passantino, and David W. Scott, *The Eye of Duncan Phillips: A Collection in the Making* (Washington, D.C.: Phillips Collection in association with Yale University, 1999), 659.

74 H. Kingston Fleming, "Part of Philips Collection on View," *Baltimore Sun*, April 17, 1927.

75 Phillips Collection, *The Phillips Collection: A Summary Catalogue.* (Washington, D.C.: The Collection, 1985), 238.; "Accession Records for Works by Charles H. Walther into the Phillips Collection, Washington, D.C.," 1927, Phillips Collection.

76 Grossman, *Art and Tradition*, 101–2; Ronald Becker, interview by Ann Prentice Wagner, June 16, 2010, Herman Maril Foundation.; David Maril, interview by Ann Prentice Wagner.

77 Herman Maril, "Letter from Herman Maril to His Cousin Maril B. Jacobs, October 18, 1980," letter, (October 18, 1980).; Oppenheimer, "Ex Parte in the Matter of the Petition of Hyman Becker for Change of Name." In his letter to his cousin, Maril stated, "'I was born Herman Becker. My mother's maiden name was Maril. When I became of legal age, I changed my name legally to Herman Maril. I had been using it as a pen name since I was 19.'" This means that Becker may have made the change to Maril in 1928, but the legal documents through which Maril changed his name in 1940 state that he began using the name Herman Maril in 1929. The self-portrait cited below, perhaps the earliest known work signed with the new name, is dated 1927-9.

78 Getlein, *Herman Maril*, 10.; Oppenheimer, "Ex Parte in the Matter of the Petition of Hyman Becker for Change of Name." Maril's petition for change of name says that he took this step "to avoid confusion with other painters having the name of Becker."

79 Peter Hastings Falk, "Herman Albert Becker," *Who Was Who in American Art, 1564-1975: 400 Years of Artists in America* vol. 1: A-F, 3 vols. (Madison, CT: Sound View Press, 1999), 257.

80 Oppenheimer, "Ex Parte in the Matter of the Petition of Hyman Becker for Change of Name."

81 Herman Maril, interview by Ronald Becker.

82 In 1925, Claribel Cone acquired her first painting by Cézanne, *Mont Sainte-Victoire Seen from the Bibémus Quarry*; in 1926 Etta Cone bought *Bathers*. See Richardson, Ameringer, and Baltimore Museum of Art, *Dr. Claribel & Miss Etta*, 175–176. Duncan Phillips acquired his version of *Mont Sainte-Victoire* in 1925. See Phillips, Passantino, and Scott, *The Eye of Duncan Phillips*, 92.

83 John Rewald and Frances Weitzenhoffer, *Cézanne and America: Dealers, Collectors, Artists and Critics 1891-1921* (Princeton, NJ: Princeton University Press, 1989); Paul Cézanne et al., *Cézanne and American Modernism* (Montclair, NJ, Baltimore, MD, New Haven, CT: Montclair Art Museum, Baltimore Museum of Art, and Yale University Press, 2009).

84 Roger Eliot Fry, *Cézanne: A Study of His Development* (New York: Noonday Press, 1958); Herman Maril, interview by Ronald Becker. Maril recalled that he had read Fry's book when he was sixteen or seventeen. This was inaccurate, since the book was not published until 1927, when he was nineteen, but this shows the Baltimore artist's youthful enthusiasm for his artistic hero.

85 Herman Maril, interview by Dorothy Seckler.

86 Hauptman, *Herman Maril*, 21. The war of which Maril spoke was, of course, World War I.

87 David Maril, "View Points by David Maril," accessed August 6, 2015, http://www.hermanmaril.com/Herman_Maril_Paintings/View_Points.html.

CHAPTER TWO

On his graduation from the Maryland Institute, Maril faced both monetary and creative challenges. The young Baltimorean felt unready to step onto the art world stage. Maril already took the attitude he would later state when he was a teacher, "I personally believe in solid, slow growth, rather than seeking for what will be popular."[1] Rather than creating art that would sell readily, Maril undertook a period of self-directed advanced art study. He said, "After graduating from that institution I spent a couple of years studying alone, looking at the works of the contemporary masters and the old masters and analyzing them and in reality, most of my actual learning process took place during that period."[2] He spent all the time he could observing art in Baltimore, Washington, New York, and Philadelphia.[3]

Even as he devoted himself to artistic ideals, Herman Maril had to cope with the everyday realities of life. He continued to live under his parents' roof, arousing resentment from siblings who had to make their own way in the world.[4] The atmosphere of the home may have been tense. To pay for a studio and art materials that would allow him to create in another space, the artist took a position as a janitor.[5] He recalled, "'I got a job at night and found a small room in Baltimore—$8 a month I think was the rent—where I could work. It was a struggle for quite a while. I had few hopes that I would be able to break into the art scene at that time; but I started to go up to New York on weekends to see as much as I could and perhaps to meet some people.'"[6]

Maril's art had appeared in public for the first time even before his graduation. His work was included in an exhibition held by the newly formed Society of Baltimore Independent Artists, whose president was Maril's mentor, Charles Walther.[7] Maril entered two paintings in the unjuried group exhibition, which the Maryland Institute predictably refused to host.[8] There was miscommunication and the exhibition catalog listed one of Herman Becker's entries as a head when the artist had actually changed his entry at the last minute to a still life.[9] Therefore the first mention of Maril's art in the *Baltimore Sun* was the puzzled query, "Why did H. M. Becker call a brown smear flanked by a black tobacco pipe a head?"[10] Maril must have been happy to have one hundred people attend the exhibition's opening night, where they could appreciate his art in person.[11]

The upset over the Maryland Institute's refusal to exhibit this modernist art exacerbated existing friction between the modernist and traditional art factions at the Maryland Institute. That summer, Walther's teaching contract was not renewed. The Maryland Institute's president, Henry Adams, denied to the press that the teacher's modern art style had anything to do with the action, citing instead tensions within the school's faculty.[12] However, the problems clearly had to do with the controversies over modern art raging in the Baltimore art establishment. Maril remained staunchly on Walther's side. The artist recalled, "We became good friends, even after I left, until he died as a matter of fact. I was one of his pallbearers. He was killed in an automobile accident [in 1938[13]]. But he was encouraging."[14]

In the years after his graduation, Maril's art transformed. One can at least roughly date the changes during the crucial year of 1929 by noting whether Maril signed his work "H. M. Becker" or "Herman Maril," a change that occurred late in the year. A gouache still life dated 1929 and signed "H. M. Becker" is shaped by the influence of Paul Cézanne in its simplified description of form and even in its choice of subject (cat. 2). Maril's gouache includes white drapery, a wine bottle, and fruit similar to those often depicted by the French post-impressionist master. The forms and perspective, however, are still quite naturalistic as the young artist drew upon his academic training. The open brushwork has a warm personal touch that would characterize the artist's mature work.

Maril spent the summer of 1929 in Ellicott City, Maryland. There he rented a cottage with his fellow young modern artists Walter Bohanan and Larry Rodda.[15] All three budding artists were former students at the Maryland Institute. In the historic seat of Howard County, the three painted landscapes and cityscapes. Among the paintings Maril made was *Ellicott City Bridge* (now titled *The Bridge*), which was later his first picture to be exhibited in the Baltimore Museum of Art.[16] The painting is dated 1929 and signed "H. M. Becker." An untitled charcoal drawing dated 1929 and signed "HM Becker" was probably also created in Ellicott City (cat. 1). Both images of buildings juxtaposed with hills and trees are rendered in a simplified modern style much more geometrical and polished than the still life painted earlier in the year. The brushwork and crayon strokes are tighter and the perspective more flattened. The structures are reductive box-like forms in a style aligned more with the early French cubism of Georges Braque and Juan Gris than with Cézanne. Maril's early cubist architectural works are closely paralleled by the blocky, heavily outlined paintings of the Maryland countryside and towns made by Charles Walther in western Maryland after his ouster by the Maryland Institute (fig. 5). Maril should not be taken as the only advanced young Baltimore modernist of the late 1920s and early 1930s. Paintings by some of Walther's other young Baltimore followers, such as Walter Bohanan, show a similar influence of cubism during the same era.[17]

Later in 1929, the young Maryland artist took up his new signature of "Herman Maril" as he achieved a more sophisticated cubist style. He used more flattened forms and less specific detail in his gouache still life *Long Haired Girl* (cat. 4) and his oil scene of buildings in a rural setting, *Landscape* (cat. 3). In *Landscape* the artist introduces willful distortions of form and decorative lines. In these works, Maril is serving a visual apprenticeship with the towering cubist masters Gris, Braque, and Picasso.

The influence of European modernism on the develop-

5. Charles H. Walther, *Johnson's House,* 1929, oil on canvas board, 22 x 18 in. (55.9 x 45.7 cm), The Phillips Collection, Washington, D.C.

ment of Maril's early art comes across most forcefully in his gouache and the identically composed oil painting of a *Still Life with Pitcher*, both made in 1931 (cats. 6, 7). The long horizontal composition, the intimate viewpoint, and the stripped-down cubist style are clearly derived from 1920s cubist still lifes by Georges Braque. In 1927, 1928, 1929, and 1931, respectively, the Phillips Collection acquired 1920s still lifes by Braque of fruit, napkins, and pitchers or other utensils. The Braque still life in this group that is most strikingly similar to Maril's still lifes with the pitcher, *Lemons and Napkin Ring* of 1927, arrived at the Washington gallery in the same year in which Maril made his versions of such imagery, 1931 (fig. 6).[18] It is evident that Maril studied Braque's composition closely. While Maril's paint application, exact colors, and surface details are different from those in the French cubist's work, the influence of Braque's composition, perspective, simplification of form, and his warm mood is undeniable. While Maril drew a great deal throughout his career from such European masters as Henri Matisse, he would rarely follow another artist as closely as he did Braque and Gris during this early period.

Even as they show the rapid development of the emerging artist's modernism sophistication, Maril's early works, with their small scale and frequent use of affordable graphic media, reflect the difficult financial circumstances he faced. The artist was not the only member of the family who had to struggle for income during the era of the Wall Street Crash of October 1929 that signaled the start of the Great Depression. Maril's father was also out of work. It was a stressful and anxious time for the whole family. As Maril later stated, "this was hardly the time to think selfishly of one's own ambition."[19]

Yet the struggling young artist continued his work on paper and, when he could, on canvas. He was laying the foundations of his modernist style even as the modern world he inhabited seemed to be collapsing. There may be something symbolic about the little 1930 watercolor *Fire*, showing a building enveloped in flames and smoke (cat. 5). The tiny modernist composition has minimal literal detail, but a ladder tells us that firemen are at work rescuing the unseen inhabitants. One wonders: Is this fire destroying the building, or will it and the people inside be saved? Maril must have had worries about the survival of his career, his family, and his country.

The mature Maril rarely prepared for paintings by making sketches more elaborate than the very brief visual notes we see in his 1973 ballpoint pen sketch made on the back of an envelope (cat. 59). But during the 1920s and 1930s, the developing artist often worked out compositions and details in careful sketches. A suite of sketches shows him creating many variations in compositions on the figural subjects he brought to fruition in his 1932 paintings of wrestlers.[20] In

6. Georges Braque, *Lemons and Napkin Ring,* 1928, oil graphite on canvas, 15¾ x 47¼ in. (40 x 120 cm), The Phillips Collection, Washington, D.C., Artists Rights Society (ARS), New York/ADAGP, Paris

1933, Maril made both a drawing and a painting of a massive Osage orange tree that stood in Druid Hill Park, near his family home (cats. 13, 14). The ancient tree, with its dramatic, long horizontal branch, fascinated the young artist.[21] Maril first captured the essential shapes of the tree and nearby buildings in a pen, brush, and ink drawing. He used dry brush dragged skipping over the paper to evoke the rough textures of leaves, bark, and ground cover. This is a small, early example of the wash drawings that would evolve into a major medium later in Maril's career. The artist enlarged the composition and added color in his oil on canvas rendition from the same year. The somber colors and unvarnished surface recall 1910s and 1920s European cubist paintings, but the individual drawing style of the young Baltimorean was starting to emerge.

Eventually, the economic and social pressures of the Great Depression grew so great that the artist recalled, "Well, as a matter of fact, right before the Treasury Department project began I really had to stop painting for a few months because I didn't have enough money to buy paints. When I saw in the newspaper that this project was being initiated new hope came with it."[22] The project to which Maril referred, the Public Works of Art Project, was the first of the New Deal art projects. It was designed both to provide monetary support to needy artists and their families and to provide the nation with art to inspire its beleaguered citizens.[23]

An event that would be vital to Maril's acceptance into the Public Works of Art Project in December 1933, and that would lead to a rapid cascade of career-altering events, occurred earlier in 1933. The young modernist was having a hard time showing his work. He felt that this was because his paintings were so abstract. The public saw his work infrequently, mainly in large group exhibitions of independent artists.[24] For example, a cubist landscape by Maril appeared in the exhibition of the Baltimore Society of Independent Artists at the Baltimore Museum of Art in October 1933.[25]

Maril's major break came the following month in Washington, D.C., where two of his paintings, depictions of a traveling fair side show and a landscape, were included in the second exhibition of the National Society of Independent Artists.[26] As the artist recalled, "'I won the prize for the most unpopular painting'[27].... It didn't bring me any money, but it did help me, as a few people became interested in my work and I was invited to show some of my paintings at the Studio House in Washington. This was associated with the Phillips Gallery.'"[28] A *Washington Post* review adds that Maril won the second place award twice over, his two paintings tying for the honor. The reviewer terms them both "delightful abstractions."[29] Phillips and other important art world figures may also have seen Maril's paintings when the artist made his New York exhibition debut with a little cubist still life included in the Museum of Modern Art exhibition *Painting & Sculpture from 16 American Cities*, which opened in December 1933.[30]

It must have been a thrill for Maril to catch the eye of Duncan Phillips, the man whose collection was so instrumental in shaping his appreciation of modern art. It was also crucial for his career. The Studio House opened in 1933 as a supplemental art exhibition space to the main galleries of the Phillips Collection. This short-lived additional gallery offered classes in art criticism, provided studio workspace for artists, and sponsored sales exhibitions of art by area artists.[31] Early in December 1933, Maril's paintings were already on the premises of the Studio House. Margaret Casey Gates, the executive secretary of the Studio House, wrote to the artist on December 13, 1933, sending a receipt for paintings that Studio House employees had picked up the previous week. She said, "We still like them and hope that we can sell some." She also noted, "We are all nearly crazy over here as Studio House has been made headquarters for the committee on the Public Works of Art for the District of Columbia—this new relief project for artists."[32]

This "new relief project for artists" mentioned in the letter would change Herman Maril's life and transform his career with dizzying rapidity. At a moment when destitution prevented the young artist and many of his friends and colleagues from working, this first of the New Deal art projects came to their rescue. Maril later wrote to one of the officers on the program to express his appreciation for the recognition that had come his way through his inclusion in the project. He said, "I also wish to thank you and your associates for your efforts in bringing about the Public Works of Art Project. I think this has been the greatest means of encouraging and stimulating the creative efforts of American artists, by its source of security, than anything in the history of the country."[33]

When the program was announced in December 1933, Maril did not assume he would be accepted. The head of the Project's Region 4, which included Washington, D.C., Maryland, and Virginia, was Duncan Phillips.[34] But the PWAP administrator in charge of the State of Maryland was Roland McKinney, the director of the Baltimore Museum of Art. Maril said, "Well, at that time I was more or less an abstract painter and the museum director in charge of the program in Maryland was a little leery of my work."[35] Probably McKinney was dubious about whether Maril's cubist-derived style would be broadly acceptable enough to suit the project's goal of ornamenting public buildings and parks.[36] It is also possible that other Region 4 committee members did not embrace Maril's work; they included not only Roland McKinney and the modernist advocate Dr. George Boaz, but also Hans Schuler.[37]

Maril was promptly hired on and appreciation of his art began to spread. Maril recalled, "I received a telegram [actually a letter] from a man named Edward Rowan to come over to Washington to see him—he liked my work."[38] Rowan wrote to the artist on January 23, 1934, "Yesterday in looking over exhibitions at the Studio House, in connection with the Phillips Memorial Gallery, I had the great pleasure of seeing two of your works. One in particular gave me the greatest pleasure and I determined at that time to write you a note of appreciation and encouragement…. I am very anxious to know more of your work with the idea of possibly exhibiting some of it at The Little Gallery, Cedar Rapids, Iowa, of which I am the Director. At the present time, however, I am engaged as the assistant technical director to Mr. Forbes Watson under the Public Works of Art Project and I have been told by Mr. Robert Gates that you are employed under this Project, also. I was very happy to learn that this is so and hope that within the near future I will have the pleasure of not only seeing more of your work, but of meeting you."[39] Such recognition was vital both to Maril's career and to his creative ego. The artist remembered, "It was the first time anybody expressed any interest in my work and naturally it was very exciting. I went over to Washington and met the man."[40]

Maril, still under the official name of Herman Becker, was added to the Public Works of Art Project payroll on December 29, 1933, as a "class A artist." This was the highest paid of three possible grades.[41] Maril recalled, "'This was a Godsend to me. We were given weekly salaries, which I used for materials. It made life worth living.'"[42] Maril and his fellow class A Maryland artists were paid thirty-eight dollars and twenty-five cents every two weeks until just before Maril was removed from the project on May 26, 1934, as the short-lived program was ending.[43] Rowan wrote to Maril, "Your sketch of 'Old Baltimore Water Front' (fig. 7) arrived safely in this office and I am extremely happy to report to you that it was highly praised and approved of by both Mr. [Forbes] Watson [PWAP Technical Director] and Mr. [Edward] Bruce [Chief of the PWAP]; they took as much pleasure in it as I did. We are hanging it here in the office where it will be seen by all of the Regional Directors of the Project."[44]

Maril's friends Walter Bohanan, Aaron Sopher, and Charles H. Walther were also in the program.[45] Walther had written a heart-rending letter to Roland McKinney begging to be added to the PWAP rolls, speaking of his difficulty in helping his son, who was not employed despite having two college degrees.[46] The letter is typical of those written by many artists in desperate financial need. If Maril wrote such an application letter, it is not preserved.

Maril made at least two suites of paintings for the PWAP. The first was a pair of panels about the story of Robin Hood, designed for Hamilton Junior High School in Baltimore. The Robin Hood paintings, now in the Maril Foundation Collection, are in the direct, narrative style that Maril felt was expected of him when working for public consumption. It was the other project, paintings made for the Peale Museum in Baltimore, which gained Maril glory. He painted a small sketch and a much larger finished version of this composition depicting the docks and warehouses of the Baltimore waterfront as it had been before a 1904 fire devastated much of the city.[47] It was evidently also on this project that he made two small paintings of Baltimore industrial scenes, although they are not discussed in the official government paperwork about the project.[48] The original assignment for the port scene had simply been for Maril to enlarge an antique map of the Port of Baltimore, but Maril convinced Mr. McKinney to take better advantage of his creative gifts by allowing him to depict an historical scene of his home city.[49] A list of PWAP projects in Region 4 further identifies the painting as depicting a scene from about 1820.[50] As his wife Esta Maril recalled, Herman Maril "took pleasure in looking at the architecture and changes in the city over the years. He enjoyed the harbor where he walked with his father."[51] The style of the smaller of the two Baltimore harbor paintings, now in the Smithsonian American Art Collection, is reductive and relatively modernist for an historical scene, but with the space and forms kept clearly legible. Maril rendered figures as doll-like forms with little detail or character. He was more involved with the geometric structures of the warehouses and the ship than with the people. The artist explained, "'The imagery was figurative, but I felt the abstract structure was dominant. However, since the progress was continually scrutinized by the 'committees,' it probably contained more genre elements which unconsciously crept into my work.'"[52]

Despite, or perhaps because of, the genre elements, the Peale Museum project paintings garnered Maril the greatest attention of his career thus far. The smaller three, including the two Baltimore industrial views, were chosen first to be included in a May 1934 exhibition of PWAP Region 4 at the Corcoran Gallery of Art. During this exhibition, the smaller of the two Baltimore harbor paintings was selected by First Lady Eleanor Roosevelt to hang in the White House, while Secretary of Labor Frances Perkins chose the two very geometrical Baltimore urban scenes to ornament her department's new building.[53]

The larger of the two harbor scenes had a particularly important history. As the artist recalled, "Well, to make a long story short, I got some nice breaks through working on that program because a large painting I was doing called *The Old Baltimore Waterfront* was selected to hang in [the Public Works of Art exhibition at] the Corcoran Gallery in the large group of works selected from the whole country and from that exhibit mine was one of the two paintings selected to hang at the exhibition at the old museum of modern art in New York City for which I received a pretty good amount of publicity. As a result of that, I had my first teaching job,

7. Herman Maril, *Sketch of Old Baltimore Waterfront,* 1934, oil on fiberboard, 18 ⅛ x 14 ⅛ in. (46.0 x 36.0 cm.), Smithsonian American Art Museum, Transfer from the U.S. Department of Labor

and a number of things came to pass."[54] Maril's painting was included in a touring exhibition of Public Works of Art Project works that was shown at the Museum of Modern Art in New York. His painting of the Baltimore Harbor was also reproduced in a national magazine. PWAP Technical Director Forbes Watson illustrated it in his article "A Steady Job" in the *American Magazine of Art* that appeared in April 1934.[55]

One of the other happy things that came to pass for Herman Maril was an enjoyable summer painting trip to Cape Cod with fellow Maryland PWAP artist Aaron Sopher.[56] In later years, Maril would establish a second home in Provincetown and spend time there every summer. His first visit was to Chatham, closer to the mainland. Maril and Sopher went up by bus and rented a foreclosed building, without electricity or water, for ten dollars per month as a studio. Maril, becoming acquainted with the local artists' colony regulars, began to fall in love with the Cape.[57] Maril said that he had been out of the rented studio and returned to discover a tall, distinguished man who had let himself into the studio and was admiring the newly produced art. It was Duncan Phillips.[58] Surprisingly, according to family tradition, Maril and Phillips had not actually met in person previously, despite the professional history between them. Phillips invited Maril to bring works to his home so the famous modernist collector could consider them.[59] Phillips purchased a pair of gouaches that summer.[60] By that December, this meeting would result in Phillips' purchase of two paintings of Cape Cod subjects by Maril, and he would buy many more in the coming years.[61] A crayon drawing of a boat at Chatham Harbor Cape shows the highly simplified but personalized modernism Maril employed during this important year (cat. 16), when he was suddenly achieving recognition and sales.

Duncan Phillips gladly loaned one of his new Maril gouaches to the young artist's first solo exhibition, held in Washington, D.C., at Howard University. The traditionally African American school exhibited a variety of art from around the world in their new gallery so their students could see the art, since blacks were not welcomed in many museums and galleries in the segregated city.[62] Phillips wrote to Maril, not only agreeing to this loan but also mentioning that he had purchased multiple works. The often-frugal collector praised Maril, even while he complained, "I cannot afford to make these purchases but I am doing so not only for your need but for the benefit of the Collection in which you rightly belong."[63] This was high praise, indeed.

Maril's new recognition was bringing him many opportunities to make art sales, if only to people in the tight circle of the Baltimore and Washington art world.[64] Works are listed as being on loan to Howard University from the Phillips Memorial Gallery in addition to private collections, including those of Roland McKinney, director of the Baltimore Museum of Art; Adelyn Breeskin, then-curator of prints of the Baltimore Museum of Art, where she was later director[65]; Olin Dows, the artist in charge of the Treasury Relief Art Project[66]; Charles Ross Rogers, Assistant Director of the Baltimore Museum of Art[67]; C. Law Watkins, head of the School of The Phillips Memorial Art Gallery[68]; Robert Franklin Gates, an artist who studied with Watkins[69]; and Dr. Eleanor Spencer, professor of art at Baltimore's Goucher College and a trustee of the Baltimore Museum of Art.[70] A *Washington Post* reviewer gave Maril's first one-man exhibition some of most substantial and perceptive early critical notice the budding artist had yet received. "There is a freshness of vision and a modern touch about the art of this young Baltimorean which has attracted the attention of the contemporary art world. He has the knack of reducing his paintings to a simple form without artistic subterfuge." The same article notes Maril's presence in the Whitney Biennial of 1934, marking another significant step up for the artist.[71] It was a fittingly triumphant close to the most eventful and easily the most profitable year thus far in Maril's career.

The spring of 1935 marked Maril's first appearance in the Baltimore Museum of Art's annual exhibition of Maryland artists. The author of a review in the *Baltimore Sun* trumpeted the major national distinctions claimed by a long list of these local artists without noting that a high percentage of these honors could be chalked up to Herman Maril alone. Maril would be a major presence in this exhibition for many years to come.[72] Also that spring, Maril appeared in the Corcoran Gallery's Biennial, a prominent exhibition that included both contemporary and older art works. While Maril did not rate critical notice in 1935, this would be another regional exhibition where he would be a prominent entrant for decades. On the recommendation of C. Law Watkins, some of Maril's paintings from the Biennial were included in a national traveling exhibition, bringing the young artist additional recognition.[73]

Maril, encouraged by his successes, continued exploring his own vision in search of the approach and subject matter that would be his own. It was a challenge to keep his independence when he felt so strongly the demands of New Deal officials and the local, regional, and national gallerists, curators, and collectors who now scrutinized his art. A little gouache of a nude seated near a stove hints at the continued modesty of the artist's life style, but also at his attempts to cope with a classic artistic subject with which he rarely seemed at home (cat. 15).

A personal and enigmatic image from the same era suggests the excitement and uneasiness the artist felt at this crucial turning point in his career (cat. 17). In a stark, urban composition shown without realistic details and rendered in restrained tones of brown and grey, a figure dives from a high platform into what could be Baltimore Harbor. The person appears to float, caught up in industrial smoke, rather than to plummet toward the water as he would in the real world. The little gouache drawing raises difficult questions. Where is the scene set? Who is the figure? Why would anyone jump so far down into a place in the water that we can't even see from the angle of the artist's vision? Is this symbolic of the artist's own brave leap into his artistic career at such an uncertain moment in his country's history? Maril's little gouache provides no easy answers.

Maril's national prominence rose again during the summer of 1935, when he got what he termed "a terrific break."[74] Olin Dows, chief of the Treasury Relief Project, devoted a sizeable article to the rising young artist in the *American Magazine of Art*. Dows noted Maril "says that his aim is to reduce ideas felt or seen to as simple a statement and as thorough an organization as possible. These ideas are pictorial…. His purpose is clear. There is always a point. It is expressed through an underlying geometric skeleton, an integrity of structure that I find very sympathetic. His observation is acute, but its statement is reduced to the bare necessities of expression. It is very much 'in training.' His greatest danger, as I see it, is in the exaggeration of this understatement into an arid mannerism."[75] Here was not only praise, but also critical pressure. It confronted Maril with the dilemma of whether to listen to influential voices in the art world or whether to find his own way. For an artist in desperate need of sales during the Great Depression, the answer could not be easy.

Maril's new prominence earned him a number of offers to teach art. He recalled. "I had never taught before…. the only job that I accepted was in Massachusetts, in the Berkshires, to teach at the school called The Cummington School of the Arts [Cummington, MA]. Chaim Gross was the sculpture teacher, and I was the painting teacher. And some of the students were older than I was. I was 25 [sic – he was 26]. It was a growth experience for me, because the school was a very fine school. The[re was] painting, sculpture, the dance, music, and literature. And when I had the time, I would attend the classes in literature, play reading. But as I say, it was an education for me. And some of my students in painting have really been going further. I did it for six summers." Maril taught at the Cummington School of the Arts at its idyllic setting in the Berkshires every summer from 1935 until 1940.[76] The school had been founded by musician and teacher Katharine Frazier in 1922 as the Playhouse in the Hills, set at a farm she had purchased in 1920. The facility and its educational offerings expanded to include plays and concerts. In 1930 the Playhouse in the Hills became the Cummington School of the Arts, and in 1931 visual arts joined the offerings.[77]

Maril's experience at Cummington was transformative. The city boy got to know the country as a place for creativity. At the school, Maril became involved in a variety of arts as he never had been before. He met and worked with important figures such as his fellow art teacher Chaim Gross. In 1938, Maril met and befriended the poet William Bronk, who had been invited to spend a week at Cummington and present his Dartmouth graduation address.[78] The next year, Bronk joined the faculty. The painter and poet wrote letters back and forth about creative concerns for the rest of their lives.[79]

Maril's joy about the Cummington experience infuses the drawings and paintings he made there (cats. 8–12).[80] He created a sketchbook stuffed with doodles among many depictions of the faculty, students, activities, and buildings. He also drew and painted the rural setting he came to love. Maril's confidence blossomed at Cummington. His painting of *Thayer's Barns* (cat. 9) is no longer dependent on other modernists. It is pure Maril in its spare, strong composition and warm use of line and color.

In his Cummington sketchbook, Maril's drawings of informally posing models in the nude give us some evidence of how the beginning art teacher ran his classes. His nudes are far from rigorously academic, but Maril did feel that the human figure was vital for art instruction. The most prominent artist to study with Maril at Cummington was the photographer Diane Arbus; however, in the summer of 1938 she spent more of her time enjoying fellow students than painting.[81] Learning to teach and gaining confidence in his abilities in that area were crucial to Herman Maril, for both his material support and his professional self-confidence. He said, "After that first experience of teaching there [at Cummington], I took private pupils during the rest of the year…. And pretty soon I started selling."[82]

His time at Cummington made a tremendous difference in Maril's life. He later said, "I used to save up enough each summer to keep me going for a few months when I got back to the city … and I painted all the time. And I started exhibiting … at local shows and state areas shows which were held at the Baltimore Museum. And I belonged to an organization called the Baltimore Artists Union which was formed around that time and that group held exhibits, quite a few, around town."[83]

In the fall of 1936, Maril achieved another benchmark of artistic success—a one-man exhibition in New York City. He had previously shown some art works at Manfred Schwartz's Gallery 144 in New York City before the gallery closed in 1934, but this did not net Maril a solo exhibition or enough sales for the artist to mention.[84] By fall 1936, his work had been on the walls of the Frank Rehn Gallery in Manhattan for six months, but this gallery also failed to grant the fledgling artist a solo exhibition.

At last, the Manhattan dealer Marie Sterner offered Maril his chance. Maril told an interviewer, "Mrs. Sterner was not a permanent dealer. She really introduced young artists but she made connections with me with some other dealers."[85] A review in the *New York Times* said, "Marie Sterner in her role as impresario continues to bring forth talents new to the New York art lover. This week her galleries are hosts to Herman Maril."[86] It seems likely that the influential Olin Dows, who wrote the essay in the tiny exhibition catalog, introduced Maril's work to the New York gallerist. The show at the Sterner Gallery included eighteen works, most of them executed in gouache on paper. The subjects were divided between rural scenes he had seen around Cummington and western Maryland, and the coasts of Cape Cod. Dows discusses the reductive nature of Maril's modernist style and his "sensitive color and distinguished design."[87]

Working in gouache made the rising Baltimorean's art affordable so it sold well even when the Great Depression caused economic hardships for artists and collectors alike. A letter from Sterner to Maril lists the sales of eight gouaches, from which Maril cleared one hundred and fifty dollars after Sterner took her hundred-dollar fee. Duncan Phillips purchased three of the gouaches.[88]

The artist took advantage of the influx of cash by moving to New York City for a few months. As he said later, "After my first show, I stayed in New York until the money dissipated."[89] This was a vital chance to learn and to build connections. Maril's contacts in New York included such artists as Mark Rothko, Marsden Hartley, Arshile Gorky, and Raphael Soyer.[90] His first New York solo show led to many more in years to come at such commercial Manhattan venues as the Macbeth Gallery, Babcock Gallery, and Castellane Gallery.[91] Also, as Maril noted, showing in New York helped to open the door to more exhibitions in Baltimore and Washington.[92]

During the 1930s, Maril had the first prints made from his designs. His 1936 silkscreen, *The Farm*, was made under the auspices of the American Artists Group, Inc., in New York (cat. 19). This was an organization founded in 1934 to make American art affordable to the masses via Christmas cards and other prints.[93] The subject probably derives from Maril's summers teaching in rural western Massachusetts or his visits to the western area of his home state. The matte surface and rich colors achieved by the silkscreen medium, a kind of stencil printing only recently adapted by WPA printmakers from its previous commercial use, made the medium well-suited to Maril's style.[94]

Maril's work also appeared in another print medium thanks to the good auspices of his friend and mentor Adelyn Breeskin, curator of prints at the Baltimore Museum of Art. She wrote to the head of the A. Hoen & Company lithographic firm, famous in Baltimore since 1835. She introduced Mr. Hoen to "Mr. Maril, who is one of our best local artists."[95] This introduction led to a black and white lithograph (cat. 18) reproducing Maril's 1936 oil painting, *The Farm* (fig. 8). The image is hauntingly surreal, with a horse enigmatically situated among ruined buildings and a tower.

Maril commanded growing respect in his home region. Critic A. D. Emmart's of the *Baltimore Sun* said of the 1937 exhibition of the Baltimore Artists Union, "It seems to me that the honors (purely unofficial, of course) are again carried off by Herman Maril, still adeptly exploiting the most authoritatively original approach and notation of any of the local painters."[96] Maril's well-earned high standing both regionally and nationally earned him exhibition opportunities in galleries and museums. January 1937 saw Maril exhibiting commercially in Philadelphia, at Boyer Galleries. The exhibition combined oil paintings with gouaches of rural, urban, waterfront, and circus scenes.[97] In March, 1939, Maril was included in a group exhibition at the Whyte Gallery, in Washington, D.C. Maril's work would appear regularly at the Whyte Gallery until the 1950s, helping to establish him as an artist who was as important in Washington as in Baltimore.[98]

In early 1939, Maril, at the age of thirty, at last achieved the well-earned distinction of a solo exhibition at the Baltimore Museum of Art. Critic A. D. Emmart noted how strange it was that this had taken so long.[99] The local boy was making good on a national scale and his leading local institution would not ignore it. In October 1938, the museum's Jury on Local Art reported to the Administrative Committee that it recommended "Messrs. Edward Rosenfeld, Herman Maril and Herald Holmes Wrenn for solo exhibitions to be held as soon as possible."[100] The *Baltimore Sun's* glowing review of his solo exhibition noted that "Herman Maril is one of the most gifted and accomplished of Baltimore artists.... It [the exhibition] is indicative of the very considerable progress he has made in a short space of years and it will convince those familiar with his painting that Maril has by no means reached the end of his development."[101] The *Washington Post*, pointing out that Maril's work had often been seen in the nation's capital, praised Maril as "an artist of originality and taste, expressing his landscapes and occasional figure studies in strong, simplified terms."[102]

8. Herman Maril, *The Farm*, 1936, oil on canvas, 20 x 30 in. (50.8 x 76.2 cm), Herman Maril Foundation

On September 1938, Maril wrote to his friend, poet William Bronk, "I have been in a constant state of movement … reworking … some of the things that I did during the summer and 'taking stock' on the development of my work. The latter may sound funny, but that is one of the ways in which a 'rich' period leaves its mark. I can't always feel any development in myself, but after I get enough perspective, I can see whether or not there is any in my work!"[103]

Maril continued to craft his personal style in response to aesthetic influences around him, combining abstraction with observation. But he could not afford to forget the financial and political realities of the day. His work continued to pull away from European cubism and to take on narrative properties, both as shaped by his maturing personal aesthetic and to help him to appeal to the public and make sales. A good example is the moving gouache *At the Corner*, which shows a blind man sitting in front of a news stand, holding out his hand in hopes of contributions from passersby (cat. 21). While the subject tells a strong story, the urban setting is rendered in the spare, subtly colored geometry Maril favored. The same combination of storytelling and abstract strength shapes Maril's watercolors of 1940 and 1941, depicting a fireman putting out a fire and a small factory set in the countryside (cats. 22–23), respectively. The artist had come a long way from his cubist works of the late 1920s and early 1930s, but whether he was entirely pleased with the change is another question.

 Despite the prominent exhibitions and enthusiastic reviews, Maril continued to struggle financially as the Great Depression stretched on. He told his nephew, Ronald Becker, "Well, I managed to have a few private pupils, incidentally. And I was able to support myself to a degree with my private pupils and the few sales I was able to make. And to get by until the War came about—World War II."[104] During the summer of 1941, Maril and his friend Donald Coale created the short-lived Herman Maril-Donald Coale School of Painting, which taught painting from the landscape and the nude model.[105] They tried to take advantage of Maril's late 1930s success by putting his name first, but the lack of information surviving about the school suggests it had little success.

Another way that Maril survived economically during these years was through two mural commissions for the Treasury Art Project. These were for the Altavista, Virginia, Post Office in 1939 and the West Scranton, Pennsylvania, Post Office in early 1941.[106] The commissions brought Maril money and recognition; however, they also subjected him to the demands of government officials and committees. Numerous sketches and proposals were required to win and execute such commissions, and the artist had to cope with whatever demands the government chose to make (cat. 20). Flattened cubist perspective and artistic reasons for shapes and proportions were beyond the ken of some government officials. In May 1939, Edward B. Rowan wrote to Maril that while his two-inch-scale color sketch for the Altavista mural was "satisfactory and acceptable….The only suggestion offered is that the railroad tracks seem somewhat too wide from the view that you have taken to present them and the scale of the fruit trees on the left seems slightly small."[107] The modernist struggled to reconcile himself to what was expected of an artist making public murals under government auspices. He said, "The fact that the government was involved, was interested. You couldn't help but [allude to nature]—and I was trying to interpret that in the terms of [abstraction]—it was rather hard … I think even painters like Max Webber, who tried it, found it difficult [to do abstraction] then." But Maril recalled, "It was a good experience going out to these places. They both were similar in nature, in the sense that West Scranton is a depressed area, or it was at that time, in 1939 or '40…. So I've got a lot of material for paintings, myself."[108]

Among the New York dealers with whom Maril showed was Hudson Walker, who gained the young artist the vital opportunity to have his work considered for purchase by the Metropolitan Museum of Art. Walker wrote to Maril about a pair of gouaches, "*Tug in Inlet* and *In the Kitchen* are on approval at the Metropolitan now."[109] These were modest, narrative images, not representing Maril's best work of the time. However, an opportunity to be considered by so important a museum was not to be sneezed at. In August it was confirmed *In the Kitchen* was to be purchased by the museum.[110] Having a work in the collection of the Metropolitan Museum was a distinction in which Maril, his family, and friends took great pride.

As the Second World War began, Herman Maril diligently did what he could to support the war effort as a civilian. He created posters for the Office of Civilian Defense, where his friend and mentor Olin Dows was acting as a consultant.[111] In February 1942, the artist was given a purchase award in a competition held by the Office of Emergency Management for Pictures to Record Defense and War Activities, which granted him the privilege of having his work exhibited at the newly founded National Gallery of Art in Washington, D.C.[112]

In June 1942, just after he completed his West Scranton mural, the artist was drafted into the army.[113] Maril served until September 1945.[114] His military service showed him some new areas of the country, as well as a very different way of life. Assignments took him from Fort Meade in Maryland, to Fort Knox, Kentucky, and to Newton D. Baker General Hospital in Martinsburg, West Virginia. During his years in the army he rose from a private to a sergeant.[115] The artist from Baltimore was not particularly impressed by his own success. In December 1943, Maril wrote from Martinsburg to his friend Selma Oppenheimer, dryly noting, "I was made a sergeant, last week. The slight increase in salary is helpful, and the added 'dignity' is amusing."[116]

Maril found little time to make his own art outside of his army work at camouflage, illustration, and images related to military medicine. He described his service later, "I have served in the Engineers, the Tanks, and the Medics."[117] He made watercolors and gouaches documenting army life. One was *On Maneuvers*, which was exhibited at the Phillips Memorial Gallery in 1942, according to a label preserved in the artist's files (cat. 24). The gouache is rendered on red poster board that would hold up to the demands of travel and military service. The gouache *Resting* is on purple poster board (cat. 26). A Baltimore publication noted, "Herman Maril, who is one of our state's most celebrated contemporary artists … decided that when he got into the army he would devote all the time he could spare to continuing his art work. To this end, he did a considerable amount of experimenting with paint on specially prepared paper and pasteboard which would be easily portable, and accessible in camp."[118] The subjects are simple scenes of military training or structures—works he could render quickly (cat. 24–26).

Oils paintings, which took longer to make and to dry, were more challenging to manage than were works on paper. He told a friend, "Have just completed a little oil (my first in a year and a-half)."[119] During his whole service, he recalled, he completed only two oil paintings.[120] He complained, "I'm kind of disgusted at a lot of people. Mainly because it's been (and still is) a difficult adjustment for me, and I feel that (like many others), I have given up a lot!"[121] However, Maril was able to exhibit his work. Sometimes he was even given leave to attend exhibitions of his own art such as a one-man exhibition at Whyte Gallery in Washington, D.C., in December 1943.[122] His exhibition career continued apace at museum and commercial venues during his service. Maril's art was also seen in such army publications as books of *Soldier Art* published by the *Infantry Journal*.[123]

Herman Maril was serious about his service. He was keen to do all his could as an artist to help his country. He also wanted his work to have artistic significance. He wrote from Fort Knox to Edward B. Rowan, his friend from the New Deal who was then working at the Public Buildings Administration, Federal Works Agency. Maril argued, "I wish to thank you for your frank letter of June 8th. However, I still feel that I am a logical person for membership in the artists units for overseas duty. The army officers here, who have seen examples of my work, feel that I am pretty realistic in my approach. The commanding colonel of my battalion is even willing to pen a note of recommendation for me to the army officials in charge of these units … I have seen a list of some of the artists already selected for the units. I must say that many of them are far more deviating away from the objective (in their work) than I am in my work. As a matter of fact, the officers here, after seeing some pencil portraits I made of several of the men, think that I am <u>very</u> realistic and objective."[124] But Maril's appeal was in vain. He was not selected to be a combat artist.

Instead, Maril was transferred to Newton D. Baker General Hospital in Martinsburg, West Virginia. There he created posters to be used in the treatment of soldiers recovering from wounds and combat stress. Some of his works were made as physiotherapy aids for such treatments as stretching injured limbs with atrophied muscles (fig. 9).[125] Other images Maril made were used in treating soldiers with psychological problems. These posters showed various situations with which soldiers often had to cope; the images allowed soldiers to point to pictures of traumatic problems rather than describing them verbally. For instance, a soldier frustrated by dealing with authority could point to a picture of "a private peeling potatoes while a sergeant is bawling him out. The solider is 'swallowing his anger' and it is visibly eating into his stomach, piling up suppressed desires for vengeance and possibly paving the way for stomach disorders."[126]

Maril was discharged from the army in September 1945.[127] He could have been in serious financial trouble. He recalled, "I lost all my private pupils that were angry at me. They all went to someone else. And I didn't have a dime, outside of about $35, which I was [got on] mustering out."[128] Yet his art contacts in Washington meant that the former sergeant had no trouble finding gainful employment, though he had to move to the nation's capital to do it. He lived there for about a year after the war. The artist's first employment was through Duncan Phillips. He recalled, "They immediately, as soon as I got out, offered me a temporary job as a sort of docent in the Gallery." Spending so many hours with such excellent art must have been a treat for the artist after so long devoted to military life. But this lasted for only about ten days before Maril moved on to be a teacher in the adult education program of the King-Smith Studio School, also in Washington, D.C.[129] Maril was soon showing some of his gouaches at the school. Some of these depicted his war experiences, while others made a novel foray into fantasy subjects such as the mythical flying horse Pegasus.[130] Maril taught in 1946 and 1947 at the Capitol Hill Arts Workshop, also in Washington, D.C.[131] 1946 brought the Baltimorean another solo exhibition at the Baltimore Museum of Art.[132] Despite his frustrations at being virtually unable to paint in oils and his failure to be named a combat artist, Maril had continued his career with remarkable success through the war and taken it up notable success after his discharge.

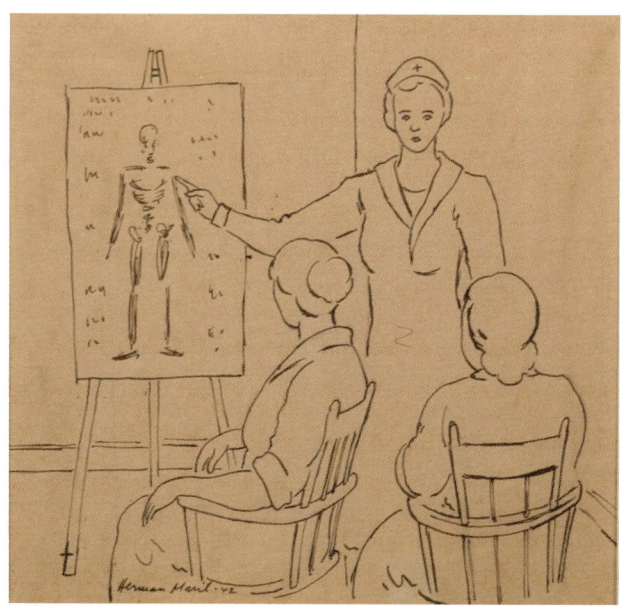

9. Herman Maril, drawing of teaching in military hospital, circa 1944, Herman Maril Foundation

Notes

1. Herman Maril, interview by Dorothy Seckler, July 5, 1965, Oral History Interview with Herman Maril, 1965 September 5, transcript, Archives of American Art, Provincetown, Massachusetts, http://www.aaa.si.edu/collections/interviews/oral-history-interview-herman-maril-11701.

2. Herman Maril, interview by Ronald Becker, July 22, 1981, transcript, Archives of American Art, Herman Maril Foundation.

3. Emery Grossman, *Art and Tradition* (New York: T. Yoseloff, 1968), 101–2.

4. Ronald Becker, interview by Ann Prentice Wagner, June 16, 2010, Herman Maril Foundation; David Maril, interview by Ann Prentice Wagner, March 15, 2010.

5. Maril, interview by Dorothy Seckler, July 5, 1965.

6. William Hauptman, "The Artist Speaks: An Interview between Herman Maril and William Hauptman," *Herman Maril* (College Park, MD: University of Maryland Art Department Gallery, 1977), 20.

7. "Independent Artists Name Their Officers," *Baltimore Sun*, May 13, 1928, sec. TM.

8. "Modern Artists' Group Finds Schuler 'Independent' Also," *Baltimore Sun*, February 4, 1929.

9. Alfred D. Charles, "From Show Card Writing to Metropolitan Museum," *Baltimore Sun*, November 3, 1940, sec. M.

10. "Independent Artists' Exhibition Draws Crowd, Baffling Many," *Baltimore Sun*, March 26, 1929.

11. "Sale of Picture Elates Independent Artists," *Baltimore Sun*, March 29, 1929, 4.

12. B. W. Sweaney, "C. H. Walther Is Ousted by MD. Institute," *Baltimore Sun*, July 30, 1929, 20.

13. "C. H. Walther, Noted Artist, Dies of Injury," *Baltimore Sun*, May 8, 1938.

14. Herman Maril, interview by Robert Brown, July 21, 1971, transcript, Archives of American Art.

15. Frank Getlein, *Herman Maril* (Baltimore, MD: Baltimore Museum of Art, 1967), 19.

16. Charles, "From Show Card Writing to Metropolitan Museum."

17. *A Stately Heritage* (Adelphi, MD: University of Maryland University College, 2000), 10–11. See Bohanan's 1929 oil painting, *Untitled (Bridge)*, given by Herman and Esta Maril to the University of Maryland, University College, in 1986. Judging from the subject and the style, this painting was probably made in Ellicott City in 1929 when the artist was painting alongside Herman Maril.

18. Duncan Phillips, Erika D. Passantino, and David W. Scott, *The Eye of Duncan Phillips: A Collection in the Making* (Washington, D.C.: Phillips Collection in association with Yale University, 1999), 248–50.

19. Herman Maril, "Speech for University College Commencement," typescript (Baltimore, MD: Herman Maril Foundation 1985).

20. 'Herman Maril: The Early Years' (Acme Fine Art and Design, November 14, 2004), not paginated.

21. CFern Shen, "Storm Fells Four-Century-Old Baltimore Tree," *Baltimore Brew*, October 30, 2012, 1-3, https://www.baltimorebrew.com/2012/10/30/storm-fells-four-century-old-baltimore-tree/.

22. Maril, interview by Ronald Becker, July 22, 1981.

23. Richard D. McKinzie, *The New Deal for Artists* (Princeton, NJ: Princeton University Press, 1973), 8–13.

24. Maril, interview by Dorothy Seckler, July 5, 1965.

25. "Independent Art Show Not Radical," *Baltimore Sun*, October 8, 1933, sec. SF.

26. National Society of Independent Artists, *Catalogue of the Second Exhibition 1933 of the National Society of Independent Artists* (Washington, D.C.: National Society of Independent Artists, 1933), 6. It is possible that this exhibition opportunity came about in connection with Charles Walther, whose work was also included in the exhibition.

27. Ibid., 3, 9. The exhibition offered a pair of bronze medals, one for the most popular work and one for the most unpopular work. Ballots to vote on both were included in the back of the printed exhibition catalog.

28. Grossman, *Art and Tradition*, 102. Maril at that time incorrectly recalled that the exhibition had been in 1930, when he was twenty-two years old.

29. "Bronze Medal Awarded to Landscape Painted by Marjorie Meurer," *Washington Post*, December 24, 1933, sec. SM, 13.

30. "Baltimoreans in N. Y. Show," *Baltimore Sun*, December 10, 1933, sec. SA.; Museum of Modern Art, *Painting and Sculpture from 16 American Cities* (New York: The Museum of Modern Art, 1933).

31. Phillips, Passantino, and Scott, *The Eye of Duncan Phillips*, 31, 609. The Studio House closed in 1938.

32. Margaret Casey Gates, "Letter from Studio House to Herman Maril about Paintings," letter (December 13, 1933), Herman Maril Foundation.

33. Herman Maril, "Letter from Herman Maril to Forbes Watson," letter (April 12, 1934), Archives of American Art, Washington, D.C.

34. Public Works of Art Project, "List of Heads of the 16 Regions, Public Works of Art Project, No. 1," Not dated, 1, Baltimore Museum of Art Archives, Public Works of Art Project, Records for the State of Maryland.

35 Maril, interview by Ronald Becker, July 22, 1981.

36 Edward Bruce, "Public Works of Art Project, Address of Edward Bruce, Secretary to the Advisory Committee to the Treasury on Fine Arts" (Congressional Record, 1934), 2, Baltimore Museum of Art Archives, Public Works of Art Project, Records for the State of Maryland.

37 Public Works of Art Project, "Region - 4, Committee Personnel," January 30, 1934, Baltimore Museum of Art Archives, Public Works of Art Project, Records for the State of Maryland.

38 Maril, interview by Ronald Becker, July 22, 1981. Maril mixed up his history a bit. Since, according to family history, he didn't meet Duncan Phillips in person until the summer of 1934, Rowan may have seen Maril's work at the Studio House rather than the Phillips Collection itself. See below where it was after the summer 1934 meeting that Phillips invited Maril to send works to the Phillips Collection.

39 Edward B. Rowan, "Letter from Edward B. Rowan to Herman Maril Commending His Art Seen at Studio House and Saying He Is Glad Maril Had Been Hired on to PWAP," letter (January 23, 1934), Herman Maril Foundation.

40 Maril, interview by Ronald Becker, July 22, 1981. Maril incorrectly remembered that he had not yet been hired on the PWAP. This was wrong, as the letter just cited proves. Also the records of his employment proved that Maril was hired on in December 1933, the first month of the PWAP, as cited below.

41 Public Works of Art Project, "Class A Artist, Becker, Hermand [Sic] M., 3810 Park Heights Ave., Baltimore, MD," May 26, 1934, Baltimore Museum of Art Archives, Public Works of Art Project, Records for the State of Maryland.

42 Hauptman, "The Artist Speaks: An Interview between Herman Maril and William Hauptman," 20.

43 Public Works of Art Project, "Class A Artist, Becker, Hermand [Sic] M., 3810 Park Heights Ave., Baltimore, MD."

44 Edward B. Rowan, "Letter from Edward B. Rowan to Herman Maril Saying His Sketch of Old Baltimore Water Front Had Arrived and Was Much Appreciated," letter (February 17, 1934), Herman Maril Foundation.

45 Public Works of Art Project, "Public Works of Art Project Pay Roll," May 27, 1934, Baltimore Museum of Art Archives, Public Works of Art Project, Records for the State of Maryland.

46 Charles Walther, "Letter from Charles H. Walther to R. J. McKinney Asking to Be Placed on PWAP Rolls," letter (December 13, 1933), Baltimore Museum of Art Archives, Public Works of Art Project, Records for the State of Maryland.

47 Ann Prentice Wagner, *1934: A New Deal for Artists* (Washington, D.C.: Smithsonian American Art Museum, 2009), 116–17.

48 "Paintings Chosen for White House," *Washington Star*, 12 May 1934.

49 Getlein, *Herman Maril*, 12.

50 "Region 4 List of Projects," 1934, 1, Baltimore Museum of Art Archives, Public Works of Art Project, Records for the State of Maryland.

51 Esta Maril, 'The Two Worlds of Herman Maril,' *Herman Maril: An Artist's Two Worlds* (Provincetown, MA: The Provincetown Art Association and Museum, 2008).

52 Hauptman, "The Artist Speaks: An Interview between Herman Maril and William Hauptman," 20–21.

53 "Paintings Chosen for White House," *Washington Star*.; "Art Is Viewed by First Lady," *Washington Post*, May 12, 1934, Herman Maril Foundation.

54 Maril, interview by Ronald Becker, July 22, 1981.

55 Forbes Watson, "A Steady Job," *American Magazine of Art*, April 1934, 179.

56 "Beach at Chatham, by Aaron Sopher," *Baltimore Sun*, November 11, 1934, sec. SA, 6.

57 Maril, "The Two Worlds of Herman Maril."

58 David Maril, interview by Ann Prentice Wagner, March 15, 2010.

59 Maril, "The Two Worlds of Herman Maril."

60 Herman Maril, "Letter from Herman Maril to Elmira Bier of the Phillips Memorial Gallery about Purchases of Art by Duncan Phillips," letter (December 11, 1934), Phillips Collection; Phillips Collection, *The Phillips Collection: A Summary Catalogue*. (Washington, D.C.: The Collection, 1985), 147.

61 Elmira Bier, "Letter from Elmira Bier of the Phillips Collection to Herman Maril about the Purchase of Two Paintings by Duncan Phillips," letter (December 10, 1934), Herman Maril Foundation; Phillips Collection, *The Phillips Collection*, 146–48.

62 "Howard to Show African Culture," *Washington Post*, February 16, 1930, 16; "Howard Exhibits Kuan-Yin Statue," *Washington Post*, November 12, 1934, 4.

63 Duncan Phillips, "Letter from Duncan Phillips to Herman Maril Agreeing to Lend Gouache *Old Mill* to Exhibition at Howard University," *Business* (12 November 1934), Herman Maril Foundation.

64 "Exhibition of Paintings in Oil and Gouache by Herman Maril, 28th November - 21st December, Howard University Gallery of Art," 1934, Herman Maril Foundation.

65 "Breeskin, Adelyn Dohme, Nee Dohme," *Dictionary of Art Historians* (The Department of Art, Art History, and Visual Studies, Duke University, 2015), (https://dictionaryofarthistorians.org/index.htm.

66 "Olin Dows, Artist Known for His Murals, Dies at 76," *New York Times*, June 7, 1981, http://www.nytimes.com/1981/obituaries/oilin-dows, artist known for his murals, dies at 76 - NYTimes.com.

67 "Museum Aide to Talk on Progress in Art," *Baltimore Sun*, January 8, 1939, sec. SO, 6.Maryland","page":"6","section":"SO","event-place":"Baltimore, Maryland","language":"English","issued":{"date-parts":[["1939",1,8]]},"locator":"6","label":"page"}],"schema":"https://github.com/citation-style-language/schema/raw/master/csl-citation.json"}

68 Ben L. Summerford, "Part I: The Phillips Collection and Art in Washington," *The Eye of Duncan Phillips: A Collection in the Making* (Washington, D.C., New Haven, and London: The Phillips Collection in association with Yale University Press, 1990), 607, 611.

69 Ibid., 618.

70 "Eleanor Spencer, 97, Medieval-Art Scholar," *New York Times*, 19 November 1992.

71 Vylla Poe Wilson, "Lithographs of Daumier, 19th Century French Painter-Caricaturist, Shown at Public Library," *Washington Post*, December 2, 1934, sec. SO, 5.

72 "Last Week of Exhibit at Museum," *Baltimore Sun*, April 28, 1935, sec. SC, 11.

73 Helen H. Campbell, "Letter from Helen H. Campbell of the American Federation of Arts to Herman Maril," letter (June 13, 1935), Herman Maril Foundation; Vylla Poe Wilson, "Fourteenth Biennial Exhibition Focuses Art World's Eyes on Corcoran Gallery Here," *Washington Post*, March 3, 1935, sec. SA, 5. Maril is not listed in any exhibition reviews, but the American Federation of Arts wrote to him later that year as an artist who had been included in the Corcoran Biennial of 1935.

74 Maril, interview by Dorothy Seckler, July 5, 1965.

75 Olin Dows, "Herman Maril," *American Magazine of Art*, July 1935, 407.

76 Maril, interview by Dorothy Seckler, July 5, 1965. The Maril Foundation Archives includes a collection of Cummington School of the Arts year books and correspondence documenting Maril's time there.

77 Adelaide Sproul, *Cummington School of the Arts: A School of the Imagination* (Watertown, MA: Windflower Press, 1991), 1–11.

78 Lyman Gilmore, *The Force of Desire: A Life of William Bronk* (Jersey City, New Jersey: Talisman House, 2006), 31–33.

79 Herman Maril and William Bronk, *Painter & Poet: The Art of Herman Maril; the Poems of William Bronk: A Collection of Letters*, ed. Sheldon Hurst (Queensbury, NY: Adirondack Community College, 2008), 5.

80 The gouache *Berkshire Huts* is probably dated 1932 in error by Maril going back later to sign and date this and *Berkshire Hills*. The style and paper of the two gouaches align perfectly, as does the pencil handwriting of the artist signing and dating them. There is no other evidence of Maril's visiting the Berkshires in 1932.

81 Patricia Bosworth, *Diane Arbus: A Biography* (New York: Alfred A. Knopf, 1984), 40–41.

82 Maril, interview by Dorothy Seckler, July 6, 1965.

83 Maril, interview by Ronald Becker, July 22, 1981.

84 Hauptman, "The Artist Speaks: An Interview between Herman Maril and William Hauptman," 20; "Manfred Schwartz, 60, Is Dead; Noted Painter and Lithographer," *New York Times*, November 8, 1970.

85 Maril, interview by Ronald Becker, July 22, 1981.

86 "A Reviewer's Notebook: Among New Exhibitions," *New York Times*, November 1, 1936, sec. X, 9.

87 Olin Dows, *Paintings by Herman Maril* (New York: Marie Sterner Galleries, 1936), 2.

88 Marie Sterner Galleries, "Letter from Marie Sterner Galleries to Herman Maril about Sales of Gouaches," letter (1936), Herman Maril Foundation.

89 Maril, interview by Robert Brown, n.d., transcript, Archives of American Art.

90 Hauptman, "The Artist Speaks," 24.

91 Maril, interview by Dorothy Seckler, July 6, 1965.

92 Maril, interview by Ronald Becker, July 22, 1981.

93 Archives of American Art, "American Arts Group Records, 1934-1965," *American Artists Group Records*, 1934-1965, accessed August 29, 2015, http://www.aaa.si.edu/collections/american-artists-group-records-6979.

94 James Watrous, *American Printmaking: A Century of American Printmaking, 1880-1980* (Madison, WI: University of Wisconsin Press, 1984), 101–2.

95 Adelyn D. Breeskin, "Letter from Adelyn D. Breeskin to Mr. Hoen about Herman Maril," letter (1936), Herman Maril Foundation.

96 A. D. Emmart, "Art - Works of the Baltimore Artists Union," *Baltimore Sun*, January 17, 1937, sec. SA.

97 Boyer Galleries, Inc., *Recent Paintings: Herman Maril* (Philadelphia, PA: Boyer Galleries, Inc., 1937).

98 "Whyte Show Opens March 30," *Washington Post*, March 15, 1939, 20.

99 A. D. Emmart, 'Art- Herman Maril Exhibition at Baltimore Museum," *Baltimore Sun*, February 12, 1939, 60.

100 Jury on Local Art, Baltimore Museum of Art, "Report of the Jury on Local Art to the Administrative Committee" (Baltimore, MD: Baltimore Museum of Art, October 17, 1938), 1, Herman Maril Foundation.

101 Emmart, "Art- Herman Maril Exhibition at Baltimore Museum," 60.

102 A. G., "Herman Maril, Harold H. Wrenn Have 1-Man Shows in Baltimore," *Washington Post*, February 12, 1939, sec. L, 6.

103 Maril and Bronk, *Painter & Poet: The Art of Herman Maril; the Poems of William Bronk: A Collection of Letters*, 11.

104 Maril, interview by Ronald Becker, July 22, 1981.

105 Herman Maril-Donald Coale School of Painting, "Advertisement and Registrar Card for Herman Maril-Donald Coale School of Painting," 1941, Herman Maril Foundation.

106 Edward B. Rowan, "Letter from Edward B. Rowan to Herman Maril about West Scranton Branch Post Office Mural," letter (January 28, 1941), Herman Maril Foundation; "Contract between the United States of America and Herman Maril, Artist," May 12, 1939, Herman Maril Foundation.

107 Edward B. Rowan, "Letter from Edward B. Rowan to Herman Maril about Altavista, Virginia, Post Office Mural Two Inch Scale Color Sketch," letter (May 27, 1939), Herman Maril Foundation.

108 Maril, interview by Dorothy Seckler, July 6, 1965.

109 Hudson D. Walker, "From Hudson D. Walker to Herman Maril Telling Him Two of His Works Are on Approval at the Metropolitan Museum of Art," letter (April 30, 1940), Herman Maril Foundation.

110 Metropolitan Museum of Art, "Letter from the Metropolitan Museum of Art to Herman Maril Saying That Press Release Would Soon Be Going out Announcing the Purchase of Paintings Including Maril's In the Kitchen," letter (August 1, 1940), Herman Maril Foundation.

111 Olin Dows, "Letter from Olin Dows to Herman Maril about Posters and Report for Office of Civilian Defense," letter (January 22, 1942), Herman Maril Foundation.

112 Edward B. Rowan, "Letter from Edward B. Rowan to Herman Maril Saying His Work Has Won a Purchase Award in the O. E. M. Competition for Pictures to Record Defense and War Activities," letter (February 5, 1942), Herman Maril Foundation.

113 Maril, interview by Dorothy Seckler, July 6, 1965.

114 "Army Separation Qualification Record Herman Maril," September 13, 1945, Herman Maril Foundation.

115 Maril's changes of rank and location can be tracked from letters to the artist from the Baltimore Museum of Art and the Whyte Gallery, among others correspondents, as well as a letter from Maril himself, in the Herman Maril Foundation Archives.

116 Herman Maril, "Letter from Herman Maril to His Friend Selma Oppenheimer about His Military Service," personal letter, (December 8 1943), Herman Maril Foundation.

117 Herman Maril, "Supplemental Statement by Herman Maril about His Military Service and Ideas for Future Art Works," September 1944, Herman Maril Foundation.

118 "About Town," *Where to Go in Baltimore*, July 10, 1942, 5, Herman Maril Foundation.

119 Maril, "Letter from Herman Maril to His Friend Selma Oppenheimer about His Military Service."

120 Maril, interview by Dorothy Seckler, July 6, 1965.

121 Maril, "Letter from Herman Maril to His Friend Selma Oppenheimer about His Military Service."

122 Kermit E. Larson, "Leave Permission for Herman Maril to Visit Washington to Attend an Exhibition of His Paintings," letter (20 December 1943), Herman Maril Foundation.

123 "Soldier Art," *Infantry Journal* (1945).

124 Herman Maril, "Letter from Herman Maril to Edward B. Rowan Asking to Be Assigned to Overseas Unit," letter, (June 13, 1943), Herman Maril Foundation.

125 "Army Separation Qualification Record Herman Maril."

126 Donald Kirkley, "Group Psychotherapy for Nervously Ill GIs," *Baltimore Sun*, December 30, 1945, sec. A.

127 "Army Separation Qualification Record Herman Maril."

128 Maril, interview by Dorothy Seckler, July 6, 1965.

129 Ibid.

130 Katrina Van Hook, "Gouaches Are Put on Display Here," *Washington Post*, December 2, 1945, sec. B, 6.

131 Maril, interview by Dorothy Seckler, July 6, 1965.

132 "3 Maryland Artists' Works to Be Exhibited," *Baltimore Sun*, September 18, 1946, 20; "Maril, Carnelli Painting on Exhibit in Baltimore," *Washington Post*, September 29, 1946, sec. S, 6.

CHAPTER THREE

Maril recalled of the new life he started in 1945, "When I got out [of the army] I went with a vengeance back to life, you know? That's when I really decided I got to paint…. Then I really looked for a real teaching job … I was single, you see, the other jobs were period jobs. Therefore I said I'm going to get a job this time. I'm going to get married. So that's when I got the job in Washington at the King-Smith School. Then from there, I got the job at the University of Maryland … I decided this is the way. I had the most time to paint. It helped me sort of evaluate. I like to get the most time to paint and getting some sort of living out of it without becoming a potboiler painter … I can look at painting this is an expression, not a means of making a living. You see this as a better way to express yourself…. Sure I'd like to sell, but I'm not going to paint something that will bring me a sure sale. Be good at teaching. And whatever you sell is the butter on the bread. You've got the bread already. To me that really is an advantage. If you depend entirely on the sale of a picture, you can't help but try to do something that might sell.'"[1]

The first basis of this new life was his teaching at the University of Maryland in College Park, beginning in the fall semester of 1946.[2] This professional relationship lasted until 1977.[3] Teaching at the University of Maryland, a position which changed from part time to full time in 1947,[4] at last gave the artist dependable financial means. Maril habitually rode a Greyhound bus from his home in Baltimore to the campus in College Park, Maryland, which allowed him ample time to think out visual ideas.[5] For most of his time teaching at Maryland, Maril compressed his classes into three days: Mondays, Wednesdays, and Fridays. This allowed him to spend Tuesdays and Thursdays, in addition to evenings and weekends, painting or spending time with his family.[6]

In addition to his art, Maril's other chief concern was family. His life was transformed by a young woman named Esta Cook. She remembered, "I first met Herman Maril when I was in high school. One of my art teachers suggested I attend an art school instead of an academic college. She thought if he [Maril] saw my portfolio he might have some helpful advice. He noted that while I had talent, it might be wise to attend college like my parents wanted. He said 'If it is meant to be, it will be.' I followed his advice. After I received my Bachelor's degree from Johns Hopkins University, I decided to become a social worker and learn more about 'life'…. Years later, I went back to thank Herman for his advice. It was the autumn of 1947 at his Baltimore studio at Fellowship House. I explained that I became a clinical social worker and this struck a chord with him. His oldest sister, Mazie, who lived in New York, was a clinical social worker and had been very supportive of his becoming an artist. We met for dinner and found we had many of the same interests. Our courtship took place in his studio…. I knew that our relationship was serious when he gave me a small painting, 'Quiet Land.' We married the following June in 1948, but delayed our honeymoon in Provincetown until August."[7]

Esta provided her husband with both financial and emotional support. (fig. 10) Her career as a social worker was as notable and important in many ways as her husband's career as an artist. Mrs. Maril was director of a Baltimore County mental health clinic before going into practical practice as a psychiatric social worker. In 1957, she began an association of some forty years with the Park School in Baltimore as a consultant who worked with students and their families.[8]

Together, Herman and Esta Maril created a warm household full of creative activity, family, and friends. In 1950, son David joined the family. In 1954, daughter Suzanne (now Nadja) arrived.[9]

The Marils' honeymoon in Provincetown, on Cape Cod, set a precedent in Herman Maril's life and career. Maril's love for the Cape had begun during his first summer there, in 1934. Said Maril, "We [he and Aaron Sopher] stayed for the summer and then went to Provincetown. That I really was excited about. The openness, the sea, the whole spirit. And it has a nice light—like in a Vermeer painting."[10] With his 1948 honeymoon, that love was renewed. From then on, the family spent most summers in Provincetown. Maril loved the peace he found on the Cape in those days. There he devoted himself to his art. He described his regime as "Oh, painting. Painting, painting. No teaching, nothing. Just painting. Even if I had to borrow money that summer I'd come up. And my kids were brought up here, ever since they were three months old. Both of them."[11]

The artist recalled the earlier years in Provincetown, "It was less hub-hub, less tension, and you could see the artists a little easier.... And you could walk in the streets and you'd meet artists." He became friends with such fellow Provincetown summering artists as Mark Rothko, Franz Kline, Karl Knaths, and Milton Avery.[12] Maril was particularly close to Milton Avery and Karl Knaths. The three artists visited each other's studios each summer. The formal and thematic affinity between their serene creations is undeniable.[13] The setting on the rock-studded shore enchanted Maril. The Cape shore and docks would figure in many of his most important paintings and drawings.[14]

The joy the whole Maril family found during their summers on the Cape is clear from the postcards Maril sent to his in-laws and his own parents back in Baltimore (cats. 27–35). The growing family is happily documented by the artist, who made little ink drawings of them fishing, sailing, and just enjoying themselves together.

Maril's exhibition career continued apace in the late 1940s and early 1950s with solo commercial exhibitions at the Macbeth Gallery in New York, as well as his longtime venue in Washington, D.C., the Whyte Gallery, among others.[15] Maril wrote to poet Bill Bronk, "I am pleased to say that my exhibition in New York [at Macbeth Gallery] was better received than any other show that I had there.... The artists in New York who came to see the show were very warm in their comments and some sent their pupils to see the exhibition.... I would like you to have seen this new work, as I believe it is quite a development from what you saw when we were in Cummington."[16] Indeed, Maril's style was changing. *The Mill*, a 1948 gouache of an industrial scene (cat. 36) is similar in its subject to the strongly outlined narrative scenes Maril had made during the 1930s and World War II. The former heavy outlines, however, were staring to break up. He used the dark ink marks as shadows and accents instead as outlines isolating forms. There is a new sense of vigorous motion in every mark.

By the time he moved on to images like his 1951 *Navigating* (cat. 39) and his 1952 *Circus Grounds* (cat. 40), his work, even on paper, was getting larger in size and broader in scope. The storm-tossed boat and the Western Maryland

10. Herman and Esta Maril in a rented house in Provincetown, 1957, photograph by Jack Miller, Herman Maril Foundation

fairgrounds both had a new abstract strength as well as a sense of lively motion. The compositions are assembled from an array of flat blocks of color. In his oil paintings like *Hurricane* (cat. 42), inspired by wreckage left by Hurricane Hazel, the growing scale, breadth, and abstraction are even more evident. If the viewer did not know the story behind the work, it would be easy to assume this painting was a pure abstraction.

Maril's evolution toward larger, more open and abstract work continued into the later 1950s and early 1960s in both oils and on paper. For instance, his 1960 casein *Gull on Red Boat* (cat. 45) is far more than a literal description of a bird perched by a dock. It is a strong, spare gathering of angular forms and strongly contrasted colors. The space is flattened and twisted in a cubist manner, played against the open sky and the expanse of the sea. *Tree Dune Forms* of 1958 (cat. 43), another drawing inspired by a Cape Cod landscape, represents an experimental approach to form. The assemblage of triangles, tipped up to fill much of the picture plane, is a new take on cubism.

Some of these changes may reflect the growing impact of abstract expressionism in the American art world. But while Maril's brushwork and colors grew more gestural and expressive, he always tied his images to the physical world and kept his compositions strongly structured. He said, "Naturally [I] had a great opportunity to see other paintings, like [Willem] de Kooning, [Jackson] Pollock…. I want to see what other people are doing. You can always learn something. And one of the influences they had on me was releasing me from certain inhibitory factors … I feel that a lot of the abstract expressionism work that I saw was a little too anarchistic and lacking in form. But the men that I respected had a good understanding of form and structure … I can see that a thing, without any reference to nature, has a context of its own in the painting itself. As a matter of fact, anybody that I looked at, I look at the abstract elements. And I don't care how beautiful the subject. Doesn't mean anything to me if it's a weak painting … It's the abstract elements that make any picture, from time immemorial. So it [abstract expressionism] didn't disturb me at all. As a matter of fact, some of these paintings had more of nature in them, than they realized."[17]

During the same period in the later 1940s and early 1950s, Maril began to make wash drawings that became a distinctive new aspect of his work. Some of these drawings, like *Figures on Shore* from a 1950 sketchbook (cat. 38), used skeins of black pen line to describe form. Even clouds were indicated with angular marks. This drawing depicts a typical Provincetown breakwater—a visual element that would recur in Maril's art for decades to come. In the 1949 drawing *Cape Harbor* (cat. 37), the artist introduced ink wash around his networks of line. *Junk*, a smaller ink drawing made in 1953 (cat. 41), reflects the same interest in abstract forms found around him that Maril explored in *Hurricane*. The angular ink brushwork is rooted in his narrative linear vocabulary of the 1930s and 1940s, but in the 1950s it grows more gestural and is less tied to traditional linear perspective.

Broader areas of brushed ink accent Maril's ink drawings of the later 1950s and early 1960s, as is seen in a lyrical depiction of his beloved *Baltimore Harbor* of 1958 (cat. 44). It is far more simplified, patterned, and geometrical than his 1934 oil sketch of the same subject. The boldly brushed wash drawing *Flower Pot by Window* of 1960 (cat. 46) reflects the continued influence of Henri Matisse, the master of modern still life, whom Maril knew so well from the Cone sisters' collection.[18]

In *Horse and Offspring* from the 1960s (cat. 47), we see a favorite subject for the Maryland artist. The importance of horses to his native state was something Maril never forgot, though he was not himself a rider. He enjoyed being taken on drives to seek out such rural subject matter. He favored both fairs featuring horses, as seen in *Circus Grounds* (cat. 40) and horses in the fields of Maryland farms as seen in this drawing. On such drives someone else would be behind the wheel; the mature Herman Maril did not drive. He took trains or buses or let others drive so he could look out the window in search of inspiration for art.[19]

As Maril developed as an artist, he also developed as a teacher. He said of the University of Maryland, "I teach two classes. One for beginners, and one of graduate students. I have the two extremes. I think the beginners' classes are a real challenge. They're kids who have just gotten out of high school—to try to tear down these early ideas that they have about art, pretty conservative, academic, tear down but rebuild in a direction which will give them a good background to go in any direction they want ... I feel that a good teacher should teach the beginners, give them good roots ... The real challenge is the beginners. The graduate students can work by themselves in most cases.... The graduate students each have their own studios and work by themselves and they make an appointment with you and they discuss their direction and you think about it.... You know, you try to clarify it for them, what they're doing."[20]

In 1955 and 1956, in addition to continuing to teach at the University of Maryland, he also taught one day each week at the Philadelphia Museum. The artist said, "I loved it, because these were serious students there ... and they painted all day long." But he did not continue this combination of mid-Atlantic teaching, saying, "But it was just too much for me, that traveling."[21]

Richard Klank, the art professor who shared an office with Maril at the University of Maryland for a few years at the end of the senior professor's career, gives insights into how Maril's teaching and his art interacted. Klank describes how Maril did not like to use sketching as an intermediate in preparation for an oil painting. He used for his own work a compositional method he also taught in classes. Perhaps inspired by the paper cutouts of Henri Matisse, he put pieces of torn paper on the surface of a canvas and moved them around to see where forms would work best. Only after that was worked out would the process of painting continue. But Maril also taught his students to evolve ideas on paper, particularly in ink wash drawings.[22]

Only as a very young artist did Maril use elaborate sketches for compositions. By the time he matured as an artist in the 1960s and 1970s, he rarely made developed sketches for paintings. He might jot down a few simple lines on the back of an envelope of another informal surface, as in his very informal 1973 ball point pen sketch *Near the Pamet* (cat. 59) to remember something he had seen. He would then develop the image in paint on canvas rather than through drawing on paper.[23] But most importantly, Maril's process of composition was mental. He said he did his preparatory studies, "'Inside [his head]. I can go into the studio and spend all of my time looking without touching the painting. Then an idea comes to me and I think about it for a long time. My mind is constantly on the problem—even when engaged in other activities. When I feel right about it, I start work.... It has to be inside before it can go outside—that is, on the canvas.'"[24]

The compositions Maril assembled in this way gained increasing appreciation in the mid-Atlantic region. In the 1950s and 1960s, and indeed throughout his career, Maril's strongest regional exhibiting presence was in Washington, D.C. Baltimore had too small a field of commercial galleries to serve Maril's needs. In his hometown, he often entered annual regional group exhibitions at the Baltimore Museum of Art and the Peale Museum, and Baltimore Art Union exhibitions. But for many years, he did not have solo exhibitions in commercial galleries in Baltimore. In 1965, an article in the *Baltimore Sun* noted that Maril had not had a solo exhibition in Baltimore for nineteen years. This was not remedied until an exhibition at Johns Hopkins University and a smaller simultaneous exhibition in the Fine Arts Building of the Baltimore Junior College in October 1965.[25]

Maril's first regular commercial gallery in Washington, D.C., was the Whyte Gallery. Having begun his relationship with the gallery with a group show of former Phillips Collection Studio House artists, he was later regularly featured in one-man exhibitions.[26] Franz Bader, who had arrived in Washington, D.C., in 1939 from his native Austria, helped to establish the Whyte Gallery.[27] In 1954, Bader became the proprietor of the Whyte Gallery, changing its name to the Franz Bader Gallery. He was anxious to make sure that Maril, one of his star artists, remained with the gallery under its new name and proprietor.[28] Bader featured Maril in the gallery's opening exhibition. Maril had frequent, though not always annual, one-man exhibitions at Bader's gallery and art bookstore for the rest of his life.[29] Maril was also a regular and respected presence at the Corcoran Biennial exhibition, a major regional exhibition for the Washington, D.C., Maryland, and Virginia area. Maril was granted a solo exhibition at the Corcoran Gallery in 1961. This fetched him a passionate rave in the Baltimore Sun by the critic and fellow modernist artist Kenneth B. Sawyer, a consistent advocate of Maril's work. Sawyer tellingly termed Maril "a lyricist in space, form, and color."[30] Maril was regularly included in the regional exhibitions mounted by the Phillips Collection from 1935 until 1961, and then in later group exhibitions in 1970 and 1976.[31]

Maril showed often outside Maryland and the District in such places as Philadelphia. Most importantly, he had a regular presence at major commercial galleries in New York City. He had four one-man exhibitions at the long time presenter of American modernism, Macbeth Gallery, from 1941 to 1951. Maril was seen in one-man shows in New York at the Babcock Gallery in 1953, 1956, and 1959. The Baltimore artist had solo exhibitions at the Castellane Gallery in 1961 and 1962. Maril was not willing to put up with desultory representation of his art. He wrote to Richard Castellane in December 1962 and broke off the commercial relationship, stating that his work was not being presented forcefully enough.[32] In 1963, Bella Fishko, of the prominent Forum Gallery, wrote to Maril, asking the artist to allow her to show his work.[33] The Forum Gallery continued showing Maril's art in New York for the following twenty years. In fact, Maril has the unusual distinction of having had continual gallery representation in New York City from the late 1930s until the present day.[34]

In the early 1960s, Maril's art continued to expand in scale and scope. The heavy outlines that had been vital parts of his visual approach since the 1920s continued to decrease in prominence in both his works on paper and his oil paintings. This is clear in an oil painting like *Driftwood*, made in 1962 (cat. 49). In such an oil painting, or a work on paper like his *Truro Weirs* of 1960 (cat. 48), the artist deployed lines more as value accents or as forms in themselves rather than as the borders of forms, although some lines retain their bordering function. Maril's brushwork developed greater sweep as his compositions grew more spacious. The artist in a 1971 interview said, "My paintings have a lot of open spaces. I like to relate these open spaces to more complex little areas."[35] During the early to mid-1960s, Maril's visual spaces and swaths of color expanded and achieved a new quietude.

During the same period, Maril's wash drawings made in ink or black watercolor become more painting-like. He no longer drew much in line, but rather he worked in broad black washes. He worked on larger sheets of paper, giving him scope for broader and more energetic brush strokes. This is evident in wash drawings like the vigorous *The Forest* of 1972 (cat. 57), in which he worked the ink so swiftly that it frothed. The growing scope and power of Maril's work are also evidence in the elegantly composed *Construction* of 1965 (cat. 50).

While Maril rarely mentioned Asian art as an influence on his work, his long-standing visits to the Freer Gallery in Washington seem certain to have had an influence on these ink wash creations. Maril's vocabulary of forms is different than that seen in such works as a nineteenth-century landscape from the Freer, but the landscape subject matter is the same. Maril, like some Japanese masters, reduced his subjects to essential elements brought together in evocative compositions rather than precise descriptions of nature. Both Maril and the unknown Japanese creator of this painting emphasize the general forms of the land, the trees, rocks, sky, clouds, and sun or moon. Figures, for Maril, are often peripheral elements rendered in schematic form. The forms he uses to stand in for human figures change over the decades, but the compositional function remains much the same.

These characteristics come to the fore in the ink wash drawings Maril made on a 1969 trip to Mexico with his wife and daughter. They stayed for three weeks, based in Mexico City. Maril enjoyed going for early morning walks. The family also hired drivers to take them to places like the town of Taxco and sites with Mayan pyramids.[36] Sketchbooks, separate sketches, and finished drawings show Maril's excitement over what he saw in Mexico. Ink drawings like *Mexican*

Mountains with Clouds (cat. 52) show strong geometric structures and an unusually assertive use of patterns of lines and dots. Maril introduced a restricted palette of colors into ink wash drawings such as *Mexico* (cat. 53), along with the powerful geometric ink wash marks. Previously rare colors like lavender appear in Maril's art during this trip, in oil paintings as well as works on paper.

While Maril was best known for landscapes, he also created domestic scenes set in his homes in Baltimore and Provincetown. He took a Matisse-inspired look inside his dining room in the 1969 ink wash *Study for Oil Interior* (cat. 54), including a slender, schematic figure. In another affectionate domestic scene, the yard of the Marils' Provincetown house appears in *Garden at 256* (cat. 78). Perhaps Maril's most important domestic figural composition is the elegant oil painting *Dialogue at Five*, for which he made multiple studies in ink wash and in acrylic or casein (cat. 55). This richly colored composition celebrates the relaxed, enjoyable interaction the artist enjoyed with family and friends in Provincetown and Baltimore. The cocktail party shown took place at the Provincetown home of Maril's friend and former dealer, Hudson Walker.[37] During this period Maril opened up his palette to include more intense yellows, oranges, and greens in works like the studies for *Dialogue at Five* and the casein depiction of dunes on Cape Cod, *Pathway to Water* (cat. 58), and the watercolor *Head of the Meadow* (cat. 70).[38]

Maril explored favorite forms and motifs in a series of monumental wash drawings made in the 1970s and 1980s. These were often large enough for him to draw from the shoulder in sweeping strokes. The dunes, trees, weirs, and fishermen of Cape Cod appear through reductive abstract forms in works like the 1972 *Forest* (cat. 57), 1973 *Forest Figures* (cat. 61), and 1974 *Towards the Beach* (cat. 67). The simple, eternal seascape where the sea meets the sky is evoked in *Incoming Tide* (cat. 62). The gracefully drooping forms of nets in weirs used to trap fish and the heroic, upright fishermen drawing in their nets seen in *Study for Weirs* (cat. 69) and *Dragging* (cat. 68) have an elemental, timeless power. In *Cliffs and Trees* of 1976 (cat. 74), lines function more as descriptions of the implied visual gesture of forms than as outlines. The visual elements are more widely spaced, giving greater visual power to open spaces. *Cliffs and Trees* is a rare but not unique instance where Maril introduced a color other than grey or black into one of these wash drawings. On this occasion, the color is a deep blue confined to the dark ink areas describing bushes huddled at the base of the cliffs.

These were scenes the artist saw every year on the Cape, and that would have been seen there for centuries. Maril knew the fishermen, who sometimes kindly dropped off newspaper-wrapped fish at the Marils' door for the family's dinner.[39] Other wash drawings captured experiences closer to the artist's Baltimore home, as seen in *Construction in the Suburbs* (cat. 60). The geometric structures the artist had enjoyed depicting since his earliest years still recur in these works made when he was passing middle age.

The mature artist and teacher Herman Maril was an encouraging friend and mentor to many people around Baltimore. Friend and collector Irvin Greif Jr. recalls Maril as a wonderful listener who always seemed genuinely to want to know about the things that interested his younger friends. Maril helped to encourage Greif's interest in making and collecting art.[40] Another younger man whom Herman Maril encouraged was his nephew, Ronald Becker, son of the artist's brother Joseph. Becker's father was not close to his artist younger brother. But Esta and Herman Maril encouraged Ron to come over to their home frequently. In about 1964, Maril allowed Ron to write a school paper about him. The Marils' friendliness helped to lead Becker into his career working for the Smithsonian Institution.[41]

As Maril grew older and more established as a teacher, he had more opportunities for travel. In 1970 Maril spent time painting in New Mexico for a residency through the Federal Restoration Project.[42] In 1973, he took delight in a trip to Italy with Esta and their friends Bill and Louise Rowles. The trip was a celebration of the twenty-fifth wedding anniversaries of both couples. Maril was thrilled to see so many great works by artists he had admired since childhood, such as

Piero della Francesca (c. 1415 - 1492) and Cimabue (c. 1240 – 1302). The group spent the most time in Florence and Rome. The Rowles recalled that the artist was so overcome with emotion on first visiting the Florentine Baptistery that he had to go away and come back the next day.[43] Maril recorded his travel experiences in art, including the wash drawing as *Stone Tables* (cat. 63). He also made a large watercolor of *Italy—Fishing Near the Bridge* (cat. 64). As a mature artist, Maril did not give in to the temptation to include postcard-like details in these works. He assimilated new sights and presented them using his established mode of abstraction.

A 1974 trip to California to visit his daughter gave Maril a new coast to paint. He captured dramatic rocks by the sea in his 1974 casein, *California Shore* (cat. 66). A dramatic series of upright rocks off the coast at Big Sur became a favored motif for Maril, who depicted them in paintings and drawings like the ink wash *Big Sur* (1974) (cat. 65). The massive natural stone upright visual elements on the coast make interesting parallels with the man-made Cape Cod breakwaters that were so familiar to the artist (cat. 82).

In his later years, Maril continued to be open to new media and approaches to art. In 1971 and 1974, he created designs for tapestries that were woven in France in association with the Atelier de St. Cyr in Paris and the Aubusson Tapestries.[44] In the late 1970s and early 1980s, Maril created a series of watercolors and acrylics that were interpreted into silkscreens created by Massachusetts artist Mark Sherwin between 1978 and 1982 (cat. 79). Maril had seen Sherwin's work at a fundraising exhibition in Wellfleet, Massachusetts. The two artists worked closely together to choose colors and adjust shapes and textures so they could achieve the best images in a series of landscape prints. These communicated Maril's vision with Sherwin's exacting skill. At times Maril would use pieces of cut paper to indicate shapes and compositions to the printmaker, much as he did when teaching about composition.[45] Maril continued exploring the same themes in related works like a slightly later and differently composed version of *Cattails* (cat. 86).

The aging Maril looked back and evaluated his art during the long, thoughtful bus rides between his home in Baltimore and the campus where he taught in College Park. In 1971 he began a journal in which he reflected on his past work, but also gathered ideas for new art. He stated, "Even though I am not involved in the contemporary movements, nor was I ever involved in so-called abstract expressionism I have been affected in (what I feel) a good way by the presence of these philosophies or painting adventures. I feel that the presence of these movements has helped in liberating me (in a technical sense). I find that my pallet has become broadened in the use and function of color. Also, I feel that my imagery is more varied."[46]

Looking out the windows of cars and buses was a vital part of Maril's image-gathering and thinking processes. Artist Mark Sherwin recalls that one day Maril was riding in the car with friends at Wellfleet, about midway along on Cape Cod. Maril suddenly and sharply called out for the driver to stop and pull over. Everyone was worried—what was the emergency? Was Maril unwell? No, he merely wanted to study and draw a striking view he had spotted. That view of trees perched atop of triangular hill overlooking the sea is now recorded in Maril's 1975 ink wash *Wellfleet* (cat. 71).[47]

Even as he aged, Maril's style and outlook continued to evolve and expand. His work took on increasing sweep and grace along with a range of new colors. Maril's images became increasingly spacious. As the artist said in 1983, "'My preoccupation in painting has always been space. Huge open areas of space. I like to think of the concept of space. I like to deal with big, open spaces. And color. Color and space is painting.'"[48] The forms in those enlarged spaces, however, grew more basic. His composition is spare but very active in the watercolor *Orange Flats* (cat. 75). His works on paper reflect the same concerns that shaped his late oil paintings. He pared down his compositions to the most essential forms of sea, sand, grass, and sky in the monumental, transcendent painting *White Moon and Sea* (cat. 73).

An almost equally simplified approach to composition guides one of his relatively rare interior scenes, the ink wash *Sketch for* Palette (cat. 76). The image is set in Maril's small studio built on the back of the Provincetown house, with a window bringing in sunlight to illuminate his work table and palette. The planes of wall, sky, table, and palette sky come together in quiet harmony with just a few marks to indicate curtains, brushes, and blobs of paint. The image, the basis for an oil painting, speaks eloquently of how Maril conceived of his work and life during the final years of his career. The artist observed, "'The content of my canvases is a oneness made up of color and space. Painting is a matter of relationships—things relating to other things. These constant relationships are important. There must be a oneness of statement. Anything you put on a canvas must relate – and that's true of life too; it's all a relationship…. As I work, I constantly remove things from the canvas to produce a stark statement.'"[49] This same unified, reductive vision was true of his works on paper.

Achieving this peaceful unity in his life was becoming more difficult for the artist-professor as the 1970s progressed. Maril requested sabbaticals multiple times from his teaching position at the University of Maryland.[50] He began to chafe at the demands and restrictions of being a professor as his art career continued to thrive and expand. In his journal Maril let out his frustration over his often tense, demanding dealings with the university faculty and administration.[51] Maril retired from his longtime faculty position at the University of Maryland after his daughter graduated from college in 1976.[52] The chair of the Department of Art, George Levitine, wrote to Maril acknowledging and granting his request to retire in April 1977.[53] Maril's retirement came after a spring exhibition of his work at the University of Maryland.[54]

The artist happily embraced his new freedom. Maril said, "'During my last two years at the university I did all my teaching in two days. I'd get up at 4:45 a.m. and be there at 7:30 a.m. and stay all day. I would be tired, but it gave me five days a week to paint.'" Retirement transformed his life for the better. "'Now, I am more fulfilled. My painting is coming to a greater fruition because I have more time. I have a greater perspective—I am able to look at the gestalt of what I'm doing.'"[55] The artist said, "'As a man gets older and starts looking down the line, he takes his own work more seriously. I've come to like the kids in the classes, but I've invested most of my life in painting, and at this stage of the game I prefer devoting more of myself to it.'" Painting topped his list of priorities, but it was not alone on the list. "'I hope to get up to New York more and keep better touch with what's going on. Maybe, with more time, I'll just do the same things, only at a little more relaxed pace. And there ought to be more time for friends, more time to talk.'"[56]

One of the joys of Maril's retirement was working with his daughter Nadja on two children's books. Two charming little books, *Me, Molly Midnight, the Artist's Cat* and *Runaway Molly Midnight, the Artist's Cat*, narrate the adventures of Molly Midnight, one of the family's dynasty of black cats.[57] The graceful forms of Molly Midnight and other Maril family cats appeared in many paintings over the years. The books feature some existing paintings in addition to new illustrations Maril made for this purpose.

The new simplicity of his life, with his teaching past and his children grown, is reflected in the artist's late works. The familiar elements of the Cape Cod landscape are celebrated in *Back Shore*, a quiet 1982 watercolor (cat. 85) showing a simple wood structure and a single figure with a boat. The same essential elements had appeared in Maril's Cape imagery many times over the years, from the 1930s (cat. 16), and the 1950s (cat. 38) on. The graceful wash drawing *Pines at Dune Road* (cat. 84) invites the viewer to enter the artist's Cape Cod haven. In 1981 Maril made both a watercolor and an ink wash of the Cape dunes with their bristling grasses animated by the constant ocean breeze. It was unusual for the artist to use such similar compositions in two media, particularly since the ink wash is certainly not a sketch for the watercolor or vice versa (cats. 80–81).

Maril said of the scenes he painted on Cape Cod, "The horizontalness of water gives me a tremendous sense of serenity."[58] This enveloping peace characterizes many of his later images both on canvas and on paper. The appropriately titled oil painting *Silent Vista* (cat. 77) juxtaposes simple planes of sand, water, and sky. The canvas is enlivened only by a few strokes to indicate the wind and the grass. The colors are quietly harmonious, reaching across one side of the color wheel from yellow-orange to yellow to green to blue. The division of a vertical canvas into bands of horizontal color recalls the abstract expressionist paintings of Maril's friend Mark Rothko, his one-time Cape neighbor. Maril recalled of Rothko, "'He was my neighbor in Provincetown, two doors away. We became very good friends.'"[59] But there is no Rothko drama in *Silent Vista*—the work and others like it speak only of radiant joy in the familiar embrace of nature. As Maril said, "Nature has always been my source."[60]

Maril took the same elemental approach to pictorial structure in many works on paper, including the 1981 acrylic or casein *Our Breakwater* (cat. 82) that shows one of the many stone structures along the Cape Coast that stood, visually linking sea to sky. Even more reductive is *Figures at the Sea* (cat. 83), in which three human figures are reduced to tiny, dark brush marks surrounded by vast, gentle waves coming into shore under a warm sunset sky. The scene is a poetic evocation of what Maril and his family had seen and participated in countless times during their annual Cape Cod retreats.

The 1982 watercolor *Horizon* (cat. 87) is yet simpler. The waves roll quietly under a sky warmed by sunlight. There is not even a hint of figures or shore. We see only the ceaseless motion of the eternal sea.

The aging Herman Maril fell very ill in the spring of 1983. He spent months in the hospital. His recovery was difficult and lengthy. His family understood that he was at last returning to his old self only when they saw him take up his brushes again. Esta Maril wrote to Maril's dealer, Bella Fishko, of the Forum Gallery, in November 1984, "Yes, it has been a long climb back and he has now been able complete some of the things he started after his surgery with excellent results. We have not been doing too much traveling … I felt it was important for Herman to get healed before we took too many trips away from home."[61] The Marils' last major trip abroad together was to Italy and Portugal in 1985.[62]

Maril continued to paint and to draw up nearly until his final breath. A 1985 ink wash of a black bird on a branch looks as if the scene may be set in the family's lush Mount Washington back yard (cat. 88). The artist's final trip was, appropriately, to Provincetown in the summer of 1986. There, Maril became ill. At the hospital at Hyannis, Massachusetts, he succumbed to pneumonia on September 6, 1986. The late artist was warmly praised in the media, both locally and nationally.[63] Many exhibitions and publications featuring Maril's work have continued to appear around the country in the years since his passing.[64]

Maril was an individualistic artist, never part of a formal or informal group united by style or approach. His only memberships were with groups that allowed for exhibition opportunities and advocated for artists' rights, such as the Baltimore Artists Union.[65] While his contemporaries generally gravitated to abstract expressionism, pop art, or other recognized groups and approaches, Maril found his own voice and his own way. He led and interacted with artists in Baltimore and Washington, but he was inspired by American landscapes, European modernism, and his own sensibility. Like Jacob Lawrence, his conception of space was freed by cubism without being bound by it in any way. Maril created a unique visual vocabulary instantly recognizable as his and no one else's.

Throughout his long career, art on paper was crucial to Maril's career in a variety of ways, though oil paintings rightfully claim pride of place. During the 1930s and 1940s, working extensively in gouache helped Maril's art to be affordable both for him to make and for his patrons to buy during the Great Depression. In his early years, he used drawings to work out his compositions. Later on, sketches were more cursory and less central; drawing was increasingly reserved for original and finished works rather than working sketches. But sketchbooks were well suited for capturing images while traveling. He recorded many of his experiences at Cummington School for Art in his sketchbooks, and he did the same much later during trips to Mexico, California, and other locales. During his military service, working on paper and boards made art possible for Maril as he moved from base to base and coped with the demands of army life.

During the 1940s and thereafter, Maril's work on paper transformed. His ink drawings expanded and matured from sketches into large, finished works as completely realized as any works on canvas. While he made some ink sketches, these images on paper were not generally subsidiary to or preparatory for oil paintings or other media; they became a characteristic form in Maril's oeuvre.

Color works on paper in watercolor, casein, and acrylic paint emerged as an important creative arena for Maril. Again, these were independent works. The ease and directness of working on paper freed him on the necessity of dealing with large canvases and slow-drying oil paints. But these images do not constitute any kind of compromise; the different technical characteristics of media on paper opened new avenues of expression. Many of these visual ideas were not suited for another medium. The drawings, gouaches, wash drawings, acrylics, caseins, and watercolors, and prints each communicated different aspects of Maril's vision.

Herman Maril's art was warm and lyrical—full of the humanity of its creator. As the artist put it, "I want a stark statement, but a statement that is full of human feeling." He achieved this wonderfully. The different media and supports of the works are of little importance by comparison with how we as viewers respond to the art works. The emotions Maril experienced as he traveled, and as he enjoyed his time at home with his family are captured and communicated to us. His hand and eye put his love of art and life on paper. Maril said in a film, "I must say that I feel grateful for being involved with something that gives me complete joy, even with its headaches."[66]

The great Baltimore artist's works have an expressive strength that gives them resonance far outside his native city and state. His art communicates universally through touch, shape, color, and space. These images tap into the humanity of his audience. As his friend poet Bill Bronk said in tribute to Herman Maril, "The sweet laughter, the gentleness, in Herman Maril's paintings is not applied to them but in the true sweetness of our experience. In the same way, their structures are also pervasive: the strong forms of our experience which we feel."[67]

Notes

1 Herman Maril, interview by Robert Brown, July 21, 1971, oral history interview with Herman Maril, transcript, Archives of American Art.

2 "Two Teachers Added at University," *Baltimore Sun*, September 16, 1946, 15.

3 George Levitine, "Letter from George Levitine to Herman Maril Acknowledging His Request to Retire from Teaching at the University of Maryland," letter (April 19, 1977), Herman Maril Foundation.Business, (19 April 1977

4 Frank Getlein, *Herman Maril* (Baltimore, MD: Baltimore Museum of Art, 1967), 20.

5 Herman Maril, "Herman Maril Journal," 1971 and 1983, Herman Maril Foundation.

6 David Maril, interview by Ann Prentice Wagner, May 20, 2016.

7 Esta Maril, "The Two Worlds of Herman Maril," *Herman Maril: An Artist's Two Worlds* (Provincetown, MA: The Provincetown Art Association and Museum, 2008).

8 Kelly Jacques, "Esta Maril: The Longtime Park School Social Work Consultant Acted as Curator of Her Husband's Artwork, Archives," *Baltimore Sun*, April 26, 2009, sec. A, 28.

9 Getlein, *Herman Maril*, 20.

10 Susan Baer, "Herman Maril--Developing and Working," *Baltimore Sun Magazine*, March 5, 1983.

11 Maril, interview by Robert Brown, July 21, 1971.

12 Ibid.

13 "Cross Currents: Milton Avery, Karl Knaths, Herman Maril" (David Findlay Jr. Fine Art, January 6, 2007).

14 Getlein, *Herman Maril*, 2, 20.

15 James Herring, *Herman Maril* (New York: Macbeth Galleries, 1948).; Jane Watson Crane, "Paintings at the Whyte Gallery: Conviction Is Byword for Maril," *Washington Post*, February 13, 1949, sec. L, 5.; Macbeth Galleries, *Herman Maril: Paintings* (New York: Macbeth Galleries, 1951).; D. R. K., "Whyte's Showing Maril Work," *Washington Post*, February 1, 1953, sec. L, 5.

16 Herman Maril and William Bronk, *Painter & Poet: The Art of Herman Maril; the Poems of William Bronk: A Collection of Letters*, ed. Sheldon Hurst (Queensbury, New York: Adirondack Community College, 2008), 16.

17 Herman Maril, interview by Dorothy Seckler, July 5, 1965, oral history interview with Herman Maril, 1965 September 5, transcript, Archives of American Art, Provincetown, Massachusetts, http://www.aaa.si.edu/collections/interviews/oral-history-interview-herman-maril-11701.

18 The Cone collection passed to the Baltimore Museum of Art in 1950 as a bequest from Etta Cone upon her death in 1949. Brenda Richardson, William C. Ameringer, and Baltimore Museum of Art. *Dr. Claribel & Miss Etta: The Cone Collection of the Baltimore Museum of Art* (Baltimore, MD: Baltimore Museum of Art, 1985), 9, 153.

19 David Maril, in-person interview by Ann Prentice Wagner, May 20, 2013.

20 Maril, interview by Robert Brown, July 21, 1971.

21 Maril, interview by Dorothy Seckler, July 5, 1965.

22 Richard Klank, interview by Ann Prentice Wagner, April 12, 2010.

23 *Herman Maril* (Baltimore, Maryland: Axis Video, 1981).

24 William Hauptman, "The Artist Speaks: An Interview between Herman Maril and William Hauptman," *Herman Maril* (College Park, MD: University of Maryland Art Department Gallery, 1977), 28.

25 Cherrill Anson, "Finally, Home Is the Artist," *Baltimore Sun*, October 24, 1965, sec. D, 26.

26 "Whyte Show Opens March 20," *Washington Post*, March 15, 1938, 20.

27 Leslie Judd Ahlander, "Show Marks Bader Anniversary," *Washington Post*, March 9, 1964.

28 David Maril, interview by Ann Prentice Wagner, May 20, 2016.

29 Leslie Judd Portner, "Bader Opens a New Gallery," *Washington Post*, April 4, 1954, sec. ST, 26.

30 Kenneth B. Sawyer, "Maril Exhibition in Capital Capital," *Baltimore Sun*, April 30, 1961, sec. A.

31 "Maril In House Exh. List," undated, Phillips Collection.

32 Herman Maril, "Letter from Herman Maril to Richard Castellane," letter (December 11, 1962), Herman Maril Foundation.

33 Bella Fishko, "Letter from Bella Fishko of Forum Gallery to Herman Maril," letter (August 31, 1963), Herman Maril Foundation.

34 David Maril, interview by by Ann Prentice Wagner.

35 Herman Maril, interview by Robert Brown.

36 Nadja Maril, interview by Ann Prentice Wagner, June 19, 2011.

37 David Maril, interview by Ann Prentice Wagner, February 15, 2011.

38 Maril was interested enough in his work in the milk-based medium of casein paint to exhibit with the National Society of Casein Painters at least once. Dore Ashton, "Art: 106 Casein Painters," *New York Times*, March 13, 1959, 32.

39 David Maril, interview by Ann Prentice Wagner, July 27, 2010.

40 Irvin Greif, interview by Ann Prentice Wagner, April 5, 2010.

41 Ronald Becker, phone interview at David Maril's Mount Washington House, interview by Ann Prentice Wagner, May 20, 2013.

42 Gary Vikan, "Forward," *Herman Maril: An Artist's Two Worlds* (Provincetown, MA: The Provincetown Art Association and Museum, 2008).

43 Getlein, *Herman Maril*, 8–9; Louise Rowles and Bill Rowles, in-person interview by Ann Prentice Wagner, April 27, 2010

44 Herman Maril, "Letter to George Levitine about Tapestries," letter (January 16, 1975).

45 Mark Sherwin, in-person interview by Ann Prentice Wagner, October 8, 2011.

46 Maril, "Herman Maril Journal."

47 Sherwin, in-person interview by Ann Prentice Wagner, October 8, 2011

48 Carl Schoettler, "Herman Maril: The Confidence That Comes with Half a Century of Painting," *Baltimore Evening Sun*, March 1, 1983, sec. C, 1–4.

49 Elisabeth Stevens, "Retirement Lets Herman Maril Get It Together," *Baltimore Sun*, April 6, 1980, sec. D, 8.

50 Herman Maril, "Letter from Herman Maril to George Levitine of the University of Maryland Requesting Sabbatical Leave," letter (April 1, 1968), Herman Maril Foundation; Maril, 'Letter from Herman Maril to George Levitine of University of Maryland Requesting a Sabbatical," letter (January 16, 1975), Herman Maril Foundation.

51 Maril, "Herman Maril Journal," April 27, 1975.

52 David Maril, interview by Ann Prentice Wagner, May 20, 2016.

53 George Levitine, "Letter from George Levitine to Herman Maril Acknowledging His Request to Retire from Teaching at the University of Maryland," letter (April 19, 1977), Herman Maril Foundation.Business, (19 April 1977

54 "Public Occurrences," *Washington Post*, February 17, 1977, sec. MD, 14.

55 Elisabeth Stevens, "Retirement Lets Herman Maril Get It Together," *Baltimore Sun*, April 6, 1980, sec. D, 8.

56 Isaac Rehert, "The Need to Give Oneself More Time," *Baltimore Sun*, February 28, 1977, sec. B, 1.

57 Nadja Maril and Herman Maril, *Me, Molly Midnight, the Artist's Cat* (Owings Mills, MD: Stemmer House Publishers, 1977); Nadja Maril and Herman Maril, *Runaway Molly Midnight, the Artist's Cat* (Owings Mills, MD: Stemmer House Publishers, 1980).

58 *Herman Maril* (Baltimore, MD: Axis Video, 1981).

59 Carl Schoettler, "Herman Maril: The Confidence That Comes with Half a Century of Painting," *Baltimore Evening Sun*, March 1, 1983, sec. C, 1.

60 *Herman Maril* (Baltimore, MD: Axis Video, 1981).

61 Esta Maril, "Letter from Esta Maril to Bella Fishko," letter (November 26, 1984), Herman Maril Foundation.

62 David Maril, "E-mail to Ann Prentice Wagner with Answers to Maril Biographical Questions," email, January 7, 2016.

63 Peter Jensen, "Herman Maril, Baltimore Artist, Dies at Age 77," *Baltimore Sun*, September 8, 1986, sec. D.; John Dorsey, "Herman Maril: Baltimore Artist Captured Both the Linear and the Lyric," *Baltimore Sun*, September 9, 1986, sec. C.; Margot W. Milch and Arnold L. Lehman, "Herman Maril," *Baltimore Sun*, September 20, 1986, sec. A.; "Herman Maril, 77; Teacher, Artist; Noted for Cape Cod Landscapes," *Boston Globe*, September 13, 1986, Third Edition.; "Herman Maril Is Dead at 77; Landscape Artist and Teacher," *New York Times*, September 12, 1986, sec. D.

64 Herman Maril's estate was until recently represented by the David Findlay Jr. Gallery in New York City. The Herman Maril Foundation is administered by his son, David Maril.

65 Carol Wharton, "A Union That Doesn't Advocate Shorter Hours," *Baltimore Sun*, November 18, 1951, sec. MM, 3. This article lists Herman Maril as a member of the Baltimore Artists Union, along with Reuben Kramer, Selma Oppenheimer, Helen Ries, Eleanor Silesky, Shelby Shackleford Cox, Bennard Perlman, Grace Amberson, Elsa Hutzler, and Cecile Baer.

66 *Herman Maril* (Baltimore, MD: Axis Video, 1981).

67 William Bronk, "Untitled Tribute to Herman Maril," *Herman Maril* (College Park, MD: University of Maryland Art Department Gallery, 1977), 7.

CATALOGUE

From Becker to Maril

1. *Untitled (Town)*, 1929
Black crayon and pencil on paper

2. *Untitled (Still Life)*, 1929
Gouache and ink over pencil on paper

3. *Landscape*, 1929
Oil on board

4. *Long Haired Girl*, 1929
Gouache with ink over pencil on paper

5. *Fire*, 1930
Watercolor and ink over pencil on paper

6. *Early Still Life with Pitcher*, 1931
Gouache, watercolor, and ink over pencil on paper

7. *Table Settings*, 1931
Oil on canvas

Cummington and the Berkshires

8. *Huts in the Berkshires*, c. 1935
Gouache, ink, crayon, and pencil on olive paper

9. *Thayer's Barns*, 1935
Oil on canvas board

10. *Berkshire Hills*, 1935
Gouache and crayon with pencil on olive paper

11. *Untitled (Cummington Performance)*, 1936
Crayon on paper

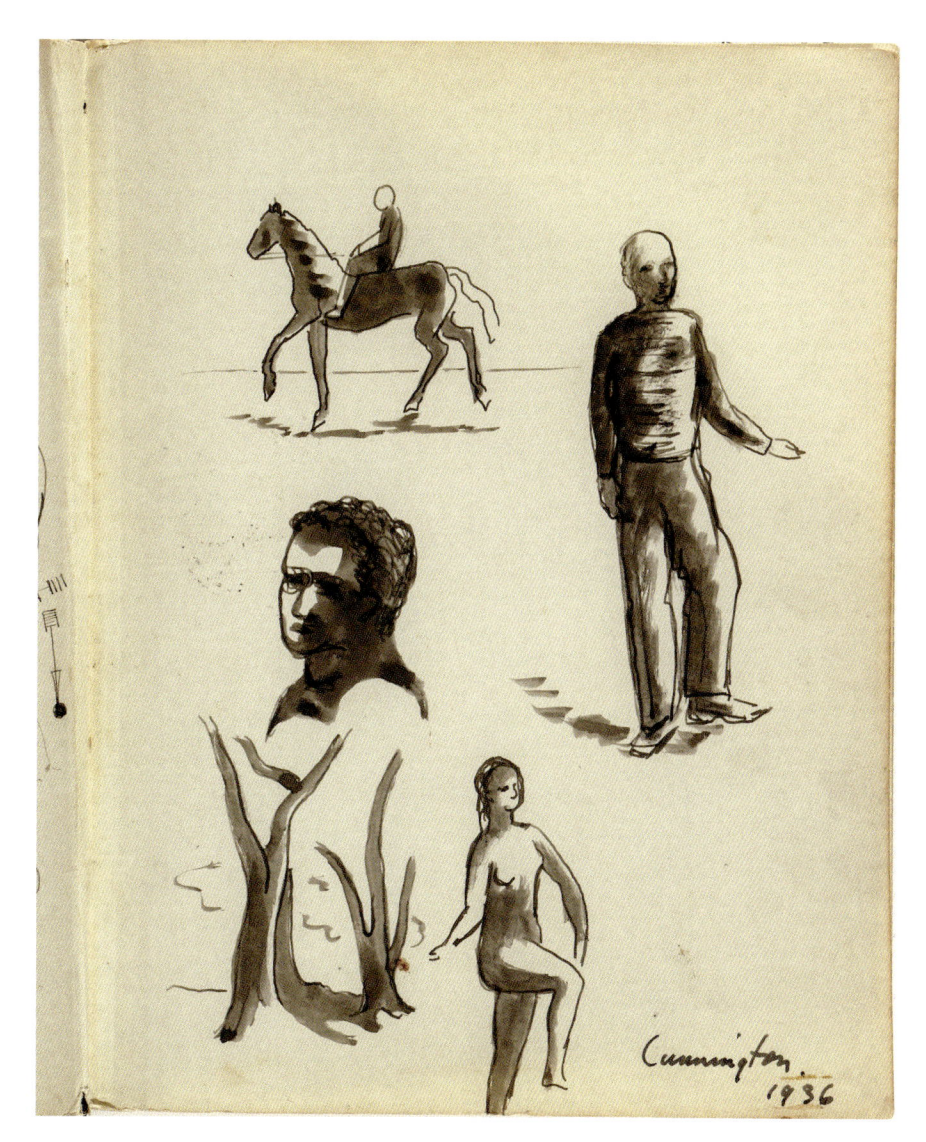

12. *Cummington Sketchbook*, 1936
Charcoal, ink wash and other media on sketchbook

Early Modernism

13. *Tree Form*, 1933
Ink wash, charcoal, and pencil on cream paper

14. *Tree Form*, 1933
Oil on canvas

15. *Nude by Stove*, 1934
Gouache and ink over crayon on cream paper

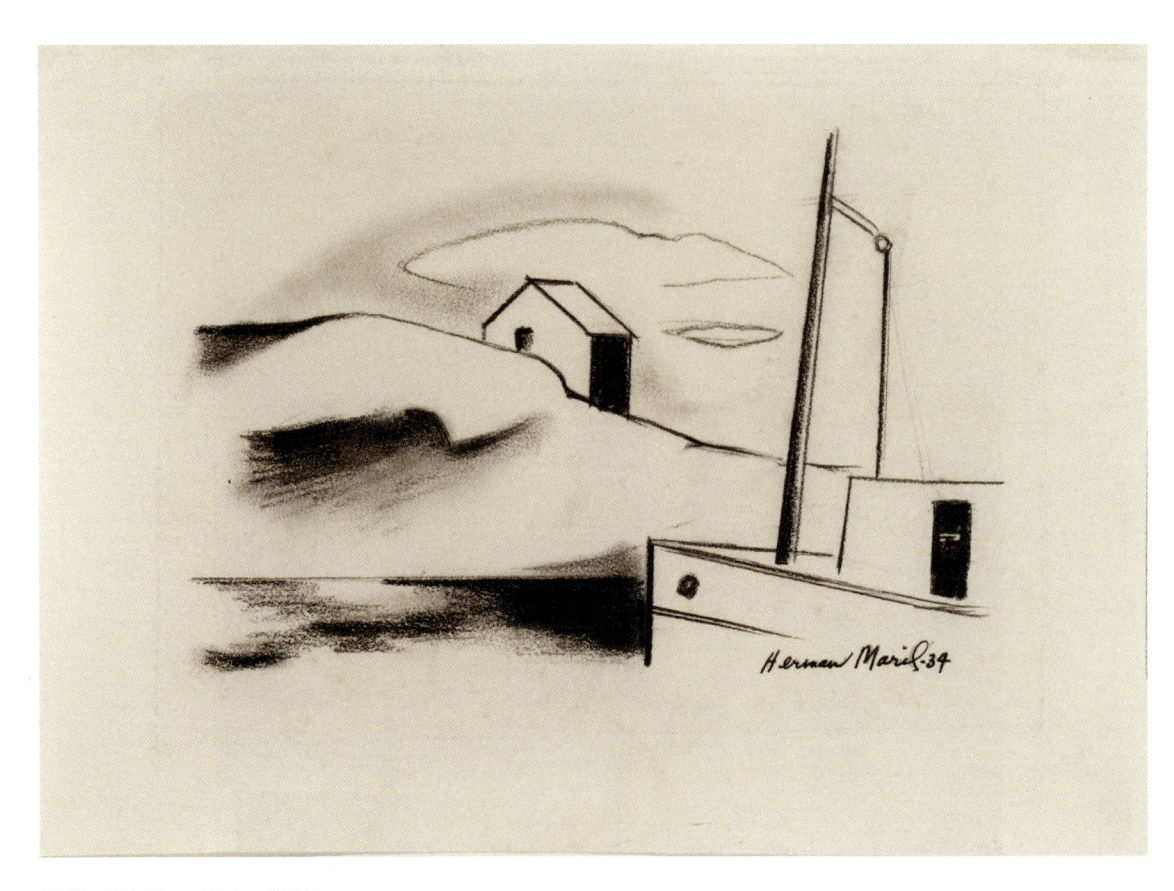

16. *Boat-Chatham Harbor*, 1934
Crayon and ink on paper

17. *The Dive*, 1935
Gouache and ink over pencil on paper or board

18. A. Hoen and Company, after Herman Maril
Untitled (Horse), 1936
Lithograph on paper

New Deal and Narrative Style

19. American Artists Group, Inc., after Herman Maril
The Farm, 1936
Silkscreen with pencil on paper

20. Study for *Alta Vista* Mural, 1937
Pen and ink, ink wash, and crayon over pencil on paper

21. *At the Corner*, 1939
Gouache, crayon, charcoal, ink, and pencil
on olive paper

22. *The Fire*, 1940
Watercolor, gouache, and ink over pencil on orange paper

23. *Little Industry*, 1941
Watercolor and gouache with ink and pencil on grey paper

World War II

24. *On Maneuvers* or *Fort Mead*, 1942
Gouache and ink on red board

25. *Barn Repair*, 1944
Ink and gouache on green paper

26. *Resting*, 1944
Gouache and ink and pencil on purple board

Postcards

27. *Postcard 1: Greetings from the Cape*, 1948
Ink on postcard

28. *Postcard 2: Having a Wonderful Time!*, 1948
Ink on postcard

29. *Postcard 3: Highland Light*, 1948
Ink on postcard

30. *Postcard 4: We Spend Our Mornings Here!*, 1948
Ink on postcard

31. *Postcard 5: Come on In!*, 1951
Ink on postcard

32. *Postcard 6: A Big Catch*, 1954
Ink on postcard

33. *Postcard 7: This is a Photo of the Olympic Swimmer, David Maril, Floating in the Ocean!*, 1957
Ink on postcard

34. *Postcard 8: You'd Better Keep Out of My Territory!*, 1960
Ink on postcard

35. *Postcard 9: David C. Maril: This is Not a Fish Story!*, 1961
Ink on postcard

Maril's New Modernism Emerges

36. *The Mill*, 1948
Ink and gouache over pencil on brown paper

37. *Cape Harbor,* 1949
Pen and ink, and ink wash over pencil on paper faced board

38. *Figures on Shore* (Sketchbook), 1950
Sketchbook with drawings in pen and ink on paper

39. *Navigating*, 1951
Acrylic or casein with ink over pencil on pink paper

40. *Circus Grounds*, 1952
Acrylic or casein with ink over pencil on paper

41. *Untitled (Junk)*, 1953
Pen and ink and ink wash over pencil on paper

42. *Hurricane*, 1954
Oil on canvas

43. *Tree Dune Forms*, 1958
Gouache and crayon on brown paper

44. *Baltimore Harbor*, 1958
Ink and brush with pencil on paper

45. *Gull on Red Boat,* 1960
Casein over pencil on brown paper

46. *Flower Pot by Window*, 1960
Ink wash with ball point pen on paper

47. *Horse and Offspring*, 1960
Ink wash and pen and ink on paper

48. *Truro Weirs*, 1960
Casein and crayon on textured paper

49. *Driftwood*, 1962
Oil on canvas

50. *Construction*, 1965
Ink and wash on paper in sketchbook

51. *The Forest*, 1967
Ink wash with pencil on paper

Explorations

52. *Mexican Mountains with Clouds,* 1969
Ink wash on paper in sketchbook

53. *Mexico*, 1969
Ink wash and watercolor with pencil on paper

54. *Study for Oil Interior*, 1969
Ink wash and watercolor with ball point pen on paper

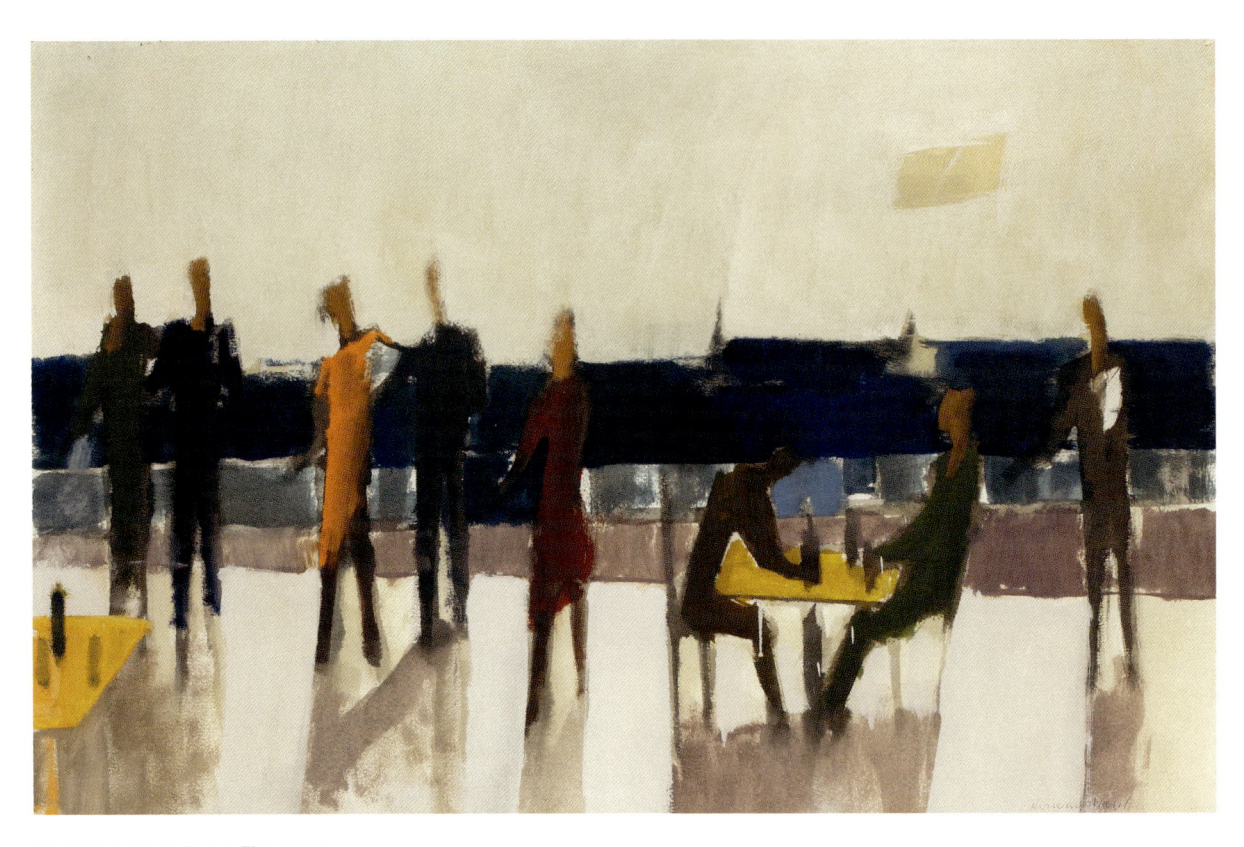

55. *Sketch for Dialog at Five*, 1970
Acrylic or casein with pencil on paper

56. *Blue Berrying,* 1971
Ink wash on paper

57. *Forest*, 1972
Ink wash with ball point pen on paper

58. *Pathway to Water,* 1972
Casein with pencil on paper

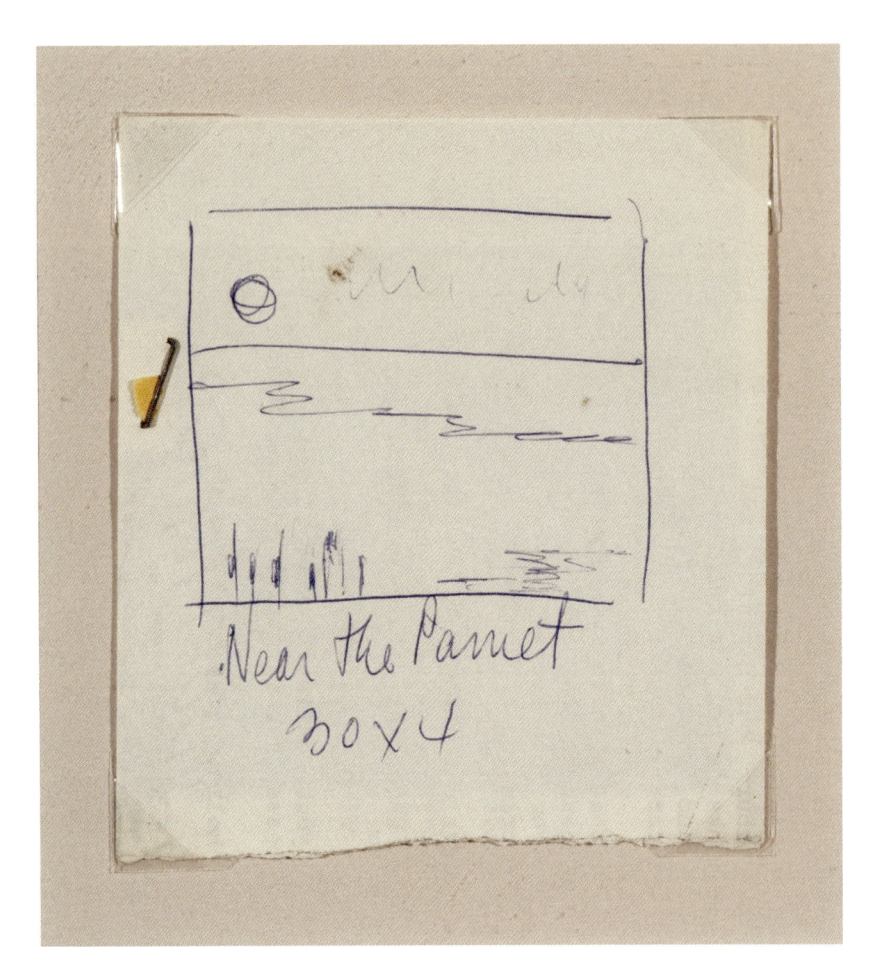

59. *Near the Pamet*, 1973
Ball point pen on envelopet

60. *Construction in Suburbs*, 1973
Ink wash with pencil on paper

61. *Forest Figures*, 1973
Ink wash on paper

62. *Incoming Tide*, 1973
Ink wash with pencil on paper

63. *Stone Tables*, 1973
Ink wash with ball point pen on paper

64. *Italy-Fishing Near the Bridge,* 1973
Watercolor and gouache or casein with ball point pen on paper

65. *Big Sur,* 1974
Ink wash and pen and ink on paper

66. *California Shore*, 1974
Casein on paper

67. *Towards the Beach*, 1974
Ink wash with ball point pen on paper

68. *Dragging*, 1975
Ink wash and watercolor with pencil on paper

69. *Study for Weirs*, 1975
Ink wash with ball point pen on paper

70. *Head of the Meadow*, 1975
Watercolor and pencil with ball point pen on paper

71. *Wellfleet*, 1975
Ink wash over pencil on paper

72. *Untitled (Construction),* 1975
Ink wash with crayon on paper

73. *White Moon and Sea*, 1975
Oil on linen

74. *Cliffs and Trees*, 1976
Ink wash and watercolor with pencil on paper

75. *Orange Flats*, 1976
Watercolor and pencil on paper

76. *Sketch for Palette*, 1976
Ink wash and watercolor with pencil on paper

77. *Silent Vista*, 1978
Oil on canvas

78. *Garden at 256*, 1979
Ink wash on paper

79. Mark Sherwin in collaboration with Herman Maril
Cattails, 1980
Silkscreen on paper

80. *Dunes*, 1981
Ink wash with pencil on paper

81. *Bluff and Sea*, 1981
Watercolor with pencil on paper

82. *Our Breakwater*, 1981
Acrylic or casein over pencil on paper

83. *Figures at the Sea*, 1981
Acrylic with pencil on paper

84. *Pines at Dune Road*, 1982
Ink wash over pencil on paper

85. *Back Shore*, 1982
Watercolor with pencil on paper

86. *Cattails*, 1982
Acrylic or casein with pencil on paper

87. *Horizon*, 1982
Watercolor with ball point pen on paper

88. *Black Bird*, 1985
Ink wash with ball point pen on paper t

EXHIBITION CHECKLIST

Section 1. From Becker to Maril

1. *Untitled (Town)*
1929
Black crayon and pencil on paper
Frame: 13 1/8 x 10 3/4 in. (33.3 x 27.3 cm)

2. *Untitled (Still Life)*
1929
Gouache and ink over pencil on paper
Frame: 13 1/4 x 10 1/4 in. (33.7 x 26 cm)

3. *Landscape*
1929
Oil on board
Frame: 20 1/2 x 16 1/2 in. (52.1 x 41.9 cm)

4. *Long Haired Girl*
1929
Gouache with ink over pencil on paper
Frame: 13 1/2 x 12 3/16 in. (34.3 x 31 cm)

5. *Fire*
1930
Watercolor and ink over pencil on paper
Frame: 13 1/8 x 10 1/8 in. (33.3 x 25.7 cm)

6. *Early Still Life with Pitcher*
1931
Gouache, watercolor, and ink over pencil on paper
Frame: 15 11/16 x 19 1/8 in. (39.8 x 48.6 cm)

7. *Table Settings*
1931
Oil on canvas
Frame: 12 3/4 x 28 11/16 in. (32.4 x 72.9 cm)
David Maril Collection

Section 2. Cummington and the Berkshires

8. *Huts in the Berkshires*
c. 1935
Gouache, ink, crayon, and pencil on olive paper
Frame: 13 7/8 x 16 5/8 in. (35.2 x 42.2 cm)

9. *Thayer's Barns*
1935
Oil on canvas board
Frame: 20 7/8 x 24 7/8 in. (53 x 63.2 cm)

10. *Berkshire Hills*
1935
Gouache and crayon with pencil on olive paper
Frame: 13 1/4 x 16 1/4 in. (33.7 x 41.3 cm)

11. *Untitled (Cummington Performance)*
1936
Crayon on paper
Frame: 13 3/4 x 16 9/16 in. (34.9 x 42.1 cm)

12. *Cummington Sketchbook*
1936
Charcoal, ink wash and other media on sketchbook
Sheet: 10 x 7 7/8 in. (25.4 x 20 cm)

Section 3. Early Modernism

13. *Tree Form*
1933
Ink wash, charcoal, and pencil on cream paper
Frame: 14 1/16 x 15 7/8 in. (35.7 x 40.3 cm)
David Maril Collection

14. *Tree Form*
1933
Oil on canvas
Frame: 17 3/8" x 20 7/8" (44.1 x 53 cm)
David Maril Collection

15. *Nude by Stove*
1934
Gouache and ink over crayon on cream paper
Frame: 15 3/8 x 12 1/4 in. (39.1 x 31.1 cm)

16. *Boat- Chatham Harbor*
1934
Crayon and ink on paper
Frame: 11 1/8 x 13 1/16 in. (28.3 x 33.2 cm)

17. *The Dive*
1935
Gouache and ink over pencil on paper or board
Frame: 17 1/8 x 13 1/8 in. (43.5 x 33.3 cm)

18. A. Hoen and Company, after Herman Maril
1936
Untitled (Horse)
Lithograph on paper
Frame: 15 3/8 x 21 1/8 in. (39.1 x 53.7 cm)
David Maril Collection

Section 4. New Deal and Narrative Style

19. American Artists Group, Inc., after Herman Maril
The Farm
1936
Silkscreen with pencil on paper
Frame: 17 3/16 x 17 3/8 in. (43.7 x 44.1 cm)

20. Study for *Alta Vista* Mural
1937
Pen and ink, ink wash, and crayon over pencil on paper
Frame: 16 3/4 x 32 7/8 in. (42.5 x 83.5 cm)

21. *At the Corner*
1939
Gouache, crayon, charcoal, ink, and pencil on olive paper
Frame: 19 3/4 x 16 1/4 in. (50.2 x 41.3 cm)

22. *The Fire*
1940
Watercolor, gouache, and ink over pencil on orange paper
Frame: 17 5/8 x 21 5/8 in. (44.8 x 54.9 cm)

23. *Little Industry*
1941
Watercolor and gouache with ink and pencil on grey paper
Frame: 20 7/8 x 27 7/8 in. (53 x 70.8 cm)

Section 5. World War II
24. *On Maneuvers* or *Fort Mead*
1942
Gouache and ink on red board
Frame: 13 ⅛ x 21 ¼ in. (33.3 x 54 cm)

25. *Barn Repair*
1944
Ink and gouache on green paper
Framed: 16 ⅞ x 23 ¾ in. (42.9 x 60.3 cm)

26. *Resting*
1944
Gouache and ink and pencil on purple board
Frame: 13 ¼ x 21 ¾ in. (33.7 x 55.2 cm)

Section 6. Postcards
27. *Postcard 1: Greetings from the Cape*
1948
Ink on postcard
3 ¼ x 5 ½ in. (8.3 x 14 cm)

28. *Postcard 2: Having a Wonderful Time!*
1948
Ink on postcard
3 ¼ x 5 ½ in. (8.3 x 14 cm)

29. *Postcard 3: Highland Light*
1948
Ink on postcard
3 ¼ x 5 ½ in. (8.3 x 14 cm)

30. *Postcard 4: We Spend Our Mornings Here!*
1948
Ink on postcard
3 ¼ x 5 ½ in. (8.3 x 14 cm)

31. *Postcard 5: Come on In!*
1951
Ink on postcard
3 ¼ x 5 ½ in. (8.3 x 14 cm)

32. *Postcard 6: A Big Catch*
1954
Ink on postcard
3 ¼ x 5 ½ in. (8.3 x 14 cm)

33. *Postcard 7: This is a Photo of the Olympic Swimmer, David Maril, Floating in the Ocean!*
1957
Ink on postcard
3 ¼ x 5 ½ in. (8.3 x 14 cm)

34. *Postcard 8: You'd Better Keep Out of My Territory!*
1960
Ink on postcard
3 ¼ x 5 ½ in. (8.3 x 14 cm)

35. *Postcard 9: David C. Maril: This is Not a Fish Story!*
1961
Ink on postcard
3 ¼ x 5 ½ in. (8.3 x 14 cm)

Section 7. Maril's New Modernism Emerges
36. *The Mill*
1948
Ink and gouache over pencil on brown paper
Frame: 15 ¹³/₁₆ x 17 ¼ in. (40.2 x 43.8 cm)

37. *Cape Harbor*
1949
Pen and ink, and ink wash over pencil on paper faced board
Frame: 18 ⅞ x 24 ⅜ in. (47.9 x 61.9 cm)

38. *Figures on Shore* (Sketchbook)
1950
Sketchbook with drawings in pen and ink on paper
Sheet: 12 ⅜ x 33 ⅝ in. (31.4 x 85.4 cm)

39. *Navigating*
1951
Acrylic or casein with ink over pencil on pink paper
Frame: 20 x 24 ¹³/₁₆ in. (50.8 x 63 cm)

40. *Circus Grounds*
1952
Acrylic or casein with ink over pencil on paper
Frame: 17 ⅝ x 23 ⅛ (44.8 x 58.7 cm)
David Maril Collection

41. *Untitled (Junk)*
1953
Pen and ink and ink wash over pencil on paper
Frame: 16 ⅝ x 13 ⅞ in. (42.2 x 35.2 cm)

42. *Hurricane*
1954
Oil on canvas
Frame: 35 ¹¹/₁₆ x 43 ⅝ in. (90.6 x 110.8 cm)

43. *Tree Dune Forms*
1958
Gouache and crayon on brown paper
Frame: 22 ¼ x 25 ¾ in. (56.5 x 65.4 cm)
David Maril Collection

44. *Baltimore Harbor*
1958
Ink and brush with pencil on paper
Frame: 14 ¼ x 16 ⁹/₁₆ in. (36.2 x 42.1 cm)

45. *Gull on Red Boat*
1960
Casein over pencil on brown paper
Frame: 19 ¹/₁₆ x 25 in. (48.4 x 64 cm)

46. *Flower Pot by Window*
1960
Ink wash with ball point pen on paper
Frame: 23 ⅜ x 16 ⅞ in. (59.4 x 42.9 cm)

47. *Horse and Offspring*
1960
Ink wash and pen and ink on paper
Frame: 16 ⅞ x 22 ⅝ (42.9 x 57.5 cm)

48. *Truro Weirs*
1960
Casein and crayon on textured paper
Frame: 33 ⅝ x 41 ½ in. (85.4 x 105.4 cm)

49. *Driftwood*
1962
Oil on canvas
Frame: 31 ⅜ x 41 ⁷/₁₆ in. (79.7 x 105.3 cm)

50. *Construction*
1965
Ink and wash on paper in sketchbook
Sheet: 11 x 28 ³/₁₆ in. (27.9 x 71.6 cm)

51. *The Forest*
1967
Ink wash with pencil on paper
Frame: 19 ¾ x 25 in. (50.2 x 64 cm)

Section 8. Explorations
52. *Mexican Mountains with Clouds*
1969
Ink wash on paper in sketchbook
Book (open): 11 x 28 ⅜ in. (27.9 x 72.1 cm)

53. *Mexico*
1969
Ink wash and watercolor with pencil on paper
Frame: 18 7/8 x 21 7/16 in. (47.9 x 54.5 cm)

54. *Study for Oil Interior*
1969
Ink wash and watercolor with ball point pen on paper
Frame: 22 3/8 x 29 5/8 in. (56.8 x 75.2 cm)

55. *Sketch for Dialog at Five*
1970
Acrylic or casein with pencil on paper
Frame: 28 1/4 x 38 3/4 in. (71.8 x 98.4 cm)

56. *Blue Berrying*
1971
Ink wash on paper
Frame: 22 3/8 x 27 1/8 in. (56.8 x 68.9 cm)

57. *Forest*
1972
Ink wash with ball point pen on paper
Frame: 30 7/8 x 37 1/8 in. (78.4 x 94.3 cm)

58. *Pathway to Water*
1972
Casein with pencil on paper
Frame: 18 1/8 x 26 7/8 in. (46 x 68.3 cm)

59. *Near the Pamet*
1973
Ball point pen on envelope
Frame: 11 1/2 x 11 in. (29.2 x 27.9 cm)

60. *Construction in Suburbs*
1973
Ink wash with pencil on paper
Frame: 22 1/8 x 29 1/8 in. (56.2 x 74 cm)

61. *Forest Figures*
1973
Ink wash on paper
Frame: 27 7/16 x 34 7/8 in. (69.7 x 88.6 cm)

62. *Incoming Tide*
1973
Ink wash with pencil on paper
Frame: 22 9/16 x 32 1/4 in. (57.3 x 81.9 cm)

63. *Stone Tables*
1973
Ink wash with ball point pen on paper
Frame: 28 5/16 x 23 1/4 in. (71.9 x 59.1 cm)

64. *Italy-Fishing Near the Bridge*
1973
Watercolor and gouache or casein with ball point pen on paper
Frame: 28 5/16 x 23 1/4 in. (71.9 x 59.1 cm)
David Maril Collection

65. *Big Sur*
1974
Ink wash and pen and ink on paper
Frame: 16 1/8 x 19 1/8 in. (41 x 48.6 cm)

66. *California Shore*
1974
Casein on paper
Frame: 22 7/8 in. x 30 7/8 in. (58.1 x 78.4 cm)

67. *Towards the Beach*
1974
Ink wash with ball point pen on paper
Frame: 22 11/16 x 32 5/8 in. (57.6 x 82.9 cm)

68. *Dragging*
1975
Ink wash and watercolor with pencil on paper
Frame: 30 1/8 x 22 7/8 in. (76.5 x 58.1 cm)

69. *Study for Weirs*
1975
Ink wash with ball point pen on paper
Frame: 16 5/8 x 19 5/16 in. (42.2 x 49.1 cm)
Nadja Maril Crilly Collection

70. *Head of the Meadow*
1975
Watercolor and pencil with ball point pen on paper
Frame: 18 7/8 x 29 1/4 in. (47.9 x 74.3 cm)

71. *Wellfleet*
1975
Ink wash over pencil on paper
Frame: 17 1/4 x 28 7/8 in. (43.8 x 73.3 cm)

72. *Untitled (Construction)*
1975
Ink wash with crayon on paper
Frame: 37 1/2 x 29 1/4 in. (95.3 x 74.3 cm)

73. *White Moon and Sea*
1975
Oil on linen
Frame: 61 1/4 x 41 1/4 in. (155.6 x 104.8 cm)
Justin Patrick Collection

74. *Cliffs and Trees*
1976
Ink wash and watercolor with pencil on paper
Frame: 21 1/16 x 28 1/4 in. (53.5 x 71.8 cm)

75. *Orange Flats*
1976
Watercolor and pencil on paper
Frame: 25 1/4 x 31 3/4 in. (64.1 x 80.6 cm)

76. *Sketch for Palette*
1976
Ink wash and watercolor with pencil on paper
Frame: 22 3/8 x 27 1/8 in. (56.8 x 68.9 cm)

77. *Silent Vista*
1978
Oil on canvas
Frame: 41 1/2 x 31 1/4 in. (105.4 x 79.4 cm)

78. *Garden at 256*
1979
Ink wash on paper
Frame: 30 3/8 x 22 11/16 in. (77.2 x 57.6 cm)

79. Mark Sherwin in collaboration with Herman Maril
Cattails
1980
Silkscreen on paper
Frame: 27 3/4 x 33 1/16 in. (70.5 x 84 cm)
University of Maryland Art Gallery

80. *Dunes*
1981
Ink wash with pencil on paper
Frame: 16 5/16 x 20 1/8 in. (41.4 x 51.1 cm)

81. *Bluff and Sea*
1981
Watercolor with pencil on paper
Frame: 16 3/4 x 19 in. (42.5 x 48.3 cm)

82. *Our Breakwater*
1981
Acrylic or casein over pencil on paper
Frame: 30 1/4 x 38 in. (76.8 x 96.5 cm)

83. *Figures at the Sea*
1981
Acrylic with pencil on paper
Frame: 24 ¾ x 29 ¼ in. (62.9 x 74.3 cm)

84. *Pines at Dune Road*
1982
Ink wash over pencil on paper
Frame: 28 3/16 x 27 ¾ in. (71.6 x 70.5 cm)

85. *Back Shore*
1982
Watercolor with pencil on paper
Frame: 22 11/16 x 18 ¼ in. (57.6 x 46.4 cm)

86. *Cattails*
1982
Acrylic or casein with pencil on paper
Frame: 32 ⅛ x 39 ⅜ in. (81.6 x 100 cm)

87. *Horizon*
1982
Watercolor with ball point pen on paper
Frame: 20 5/16 x 17 3/16 in. (51.6 x 43.7 cm)

88. *Black Bird*
1985
Ink wash with ball point pen on paper
Frame: 24 ½ x 29 ⅜ in. (62 x 74.6 cm)

All artworks are courtesy of the Herman Maril Foundation Collection unless otherwise indicated.

CHRONOLOGY

This chronology does not include a complete listing of Maril's one-man exhibitions; only relatively significant exhibitions are included. Group exhibition are included only near the beginning of Maril's career, when they were of relative importance to him. He entered annual juried group exhibitions at the Baltimore Museum of Art and the Corcoran Gallery of Art for many years.

1908, October 13: Herman Maril is born in Baltimore, Maryland, son of Isaac Becker and Celia Maril.[1]

1920, September 1: Alon Bement is made head of the School of Art and Design at the Maryland Institute.[2]

1921: The Phillips Memorial Gallery opens in Washington, D.C.[3]

1922: Maril enters night school of the Maryland Institute, College of Art, Baltimore, Maryland.[4]

1926: Maril graduates from Baltimore Polytechnic Institute, Baltimore, Maryland.[5]

1926: Maril begins regular study at the Maryland Institute, College of Art, Baltimore, Maryland.[6]

1927: First edition of *Cezanne and His Development* by Roger Fry is published. Maril reads it soon afterward.[7]

1927, April 8–May 1 and April 12–May 3: exhibitions from the Phillips Collection *An Exhibition of Expressionist Painters from the Experiment Station of the Phillips Memorial Gallery* and *American Themes by American Painters* are shown at the Baltimore Museum of Art and at the Friends of Art, Baltimore, Maryland.[8]

1928: Maril graduates from the Maryland Institute, College of Art, Baltimore, Maryland.[9]

1928: Maril works as janitor for a small building, using this income to rent a room as a studio in Baltimore.[10]

1929: Maril's father is out of work.[11]

1929, March 23–April 14: Maril is included in an exhibition of the Baltimore Society of Independent Artists, his first exhibition outside of school shows.[12]

1929, Summer: Maril rents a cottage in Ellicott City, Maryland, with Larry Rodda and Walter Bohanan.[13]

1929, July 30: Charles W. Walther's contract is not renewed by Maryland Institute College of Art.[14]

1931: Phillips Collection acquires painting by Georges Braque, *Lemons and Napkin Ring*, 1928, and the similar *Pitcher, Pipe and Pear*, c. 1924, which inspired Maril's cubist still lifes of 1931.[15]

1932: Maril's painting is voted "most unpopular" at exhibition of National Society of Independent Artists, Washington, D.C.[16]

1933: The Studio House Gallery associated with the Phillips Memorial Gallery opens in Washington, D.C.[17]

1933, December: Maril is included in the Museum of Modern Art, New York, exhibition *Painting & Sculpture from 16 American Cities*.[18]

1934: The Artists Union of Baltimore is founded.[19]

1934, January 23: Edward B. Rowan writes to Herman Maril praising paintings he had seen by Maril at the Studio House of the Phillips Collection, Washington, D.C.[20]

1934, January 27: Maril gets his first Public Works of Art Project paycheck. He remains on the payroll until May 14, 1934.[21]

1934, February 17: Maril's sketch of *Old Baltimore Waterfront* arrives at the headquarters of the PWAP and is shown in the office. [22]

1934, April: Maril's painting *Old Baltimore Waterfront* is reproduced in the *American Magazine of Art*. [23]

1934, Summer: With Maryland artist Aaron Sopher, Maril makes first trip to Cape Cod. Duncan Phillips visits their studio and meets Herman Maril. Phillips acquires two gouaches by Maril.[24]

1934, April 23–May 20: Maril's art is included in Corcoran Gallery exhibition of PWAP works.[25]

1934, May: Maril's PWAP painting *Old Baltimore Waterfront* is chosen to hang in the White House.[26]

1934, September 19–October 7: Maril's work is included in the exhibition of PWAP works at the Museum of Modern Art, New York.[27]

1934, November 17: Sale is held of PWAP works included in the Corcoran Gallery exhibition. Maril and Walther both sell paintings to Duncan Phillips.[28]

1934, November 28–December 1: Maril's first one-man show is held at Howard University Gallery of Art, Washington, D.C. [29]

1935, April: Maril's work is included in the *Third Annual Exhibition by Painters, Sculptors, and Print Makers* at the Baltimore Museum of Art. [30]

1935, July: Olin Dows publishes an article about Herman Maril in the *American Magazine of Art*.[31]

1935, ten weeks in the Summer: Maril teaches at Cummington School of the Arts, Cummington, Massachusetts.[32]

1935: Maril's work is included in 14th Corcoran Biennial of Contemporary Art, Washington, D.C.[33]

1936, February: Maril's work is included in a group show of works from The Phillips Collection Studio House at the Boyer Galleries in Philadelphia.[34]

1936, April 1–18: Maril's work is included in exhibition at the Phillips Collection Studio House.[35]

1936, ten weeks in the Summer: Maril teaches at Cummington School of the Arts, Cummington, Massachusetts.[36]

1936, October 26–November 7: Marie Sterner gives Maril his first New York show in her 57th Street gallery. Afterwards Maril lives in New York City for several months.[37]

1937, January 27–February 16–Maril has one-man show at the Boyer Galleries, Philadelphia, Pennsylvania.[38]

1937, ten weeks in the Summer: Maril teaches at Cummington School of the Arts, Cummington, Massachusetts.[39]

1938, May 8: Charles H. Walther, Maril's teacher and mentor, dies in automobile accident at the age of fifty-nine.[40] Maril is one of his pallbearers.[41]

1938, ten weeks in the Summer: Maril teaches at Cummington School of the Arts, Cummington, Massachusetts. Maril meets William Bronk.[42]

1938: Oil painting by Maril is included in 49th Annual Exhibition of American Paintings and Sculpture at the Art Institute of Chicago.[43]

1939, February 1–19: Maril has his first one-man show at the Baltimore Museum of Art.[44]

1939, March 19–April 5: Maril's work is included in exhibition of *Young Washington Painters: Former "Studio House" Exhibitors* at the Whyte Gallery in Washington, D.C. This begins his long association with the Whyte Gallery and its successor, the Franz Bader Gallery.[45]

1939: Maril's art is exhibited at New York World's Fair.[46]

1939: Maril's art is included in Golden Gate Exposition in San Francisco.[47]

1939, May 12: Maril is contracted to paint mural for Altavista, Virginia, post office, as part of the Treasury Department Section of Fine Arts mural program.[48]

1939, ten weeks in the Summer: Maril teaches at Cummington School of the Arts, Cummington, Massachusetts.[49]

1939: Art and book dealer Franz Bader moves to Washington, D.C., from Austria. He meets Herman Maril.[50]

1940, April 3–30: Maril has one-man show at the Whyte Gallery, Washington, D.C.[51]

1940, August: Maril gets letter from Metropolitan Museum of Art about their acquisition of his gouache *In the Kitchen*.[52]

1940, ten weeks in the Summer: Maril teaches at Cummington School of the Arts, Cummington, Massachusetts.[53]

1940, November 3: Herman Maril is profiled in the *Baltimore Sun* by Alfred D. Charles.[54]

1941, January: Maril is contracted to paint mural for West Scranton, Pennsylvania, Post Office.[55]

1941, until March 16: Maril has one-man show at the Macbeth Gallery, New York.[56]

1941, June 23–August 1: Herman Maril-Donald Coal School of Painting is open in Baltimore.[57]

1942–January–Maril makes posters for Office of Civilian Defense.[58]

1942, February 9–March 15: Maril's painting *Sunday Playground* is included in *On the Bright Side*, a loan exhibition of American paintings and sculpture at the Metropolitan Museum of Art, New York.[59]

1942, February: Maril is given a purchase award in a competition held by the Office of Emergency Management for Pictures to Record Defense and War Activities. Works are shown at the National Gallery of Art, Washington, D.C.[60]

1942, April 12: American Red Cross Competition acquires work by Maril.[61]

1942, June 30: Maril begins service in the United States Army.[62]

1943, April 19–May 1: Maril has one-man show at Macbeth Gallery, New York.[63]

1943, June 23: Maril writes a letter to the editor of the *Baltimore Evening Sun* decrying the end of the WPA Federal Art Project.[64]

1943, October 27–December 12: Maril's painting *East Baltimore* is included in the *54th Annual Exhibition of American Paintings and Sculpture* at the Art Institute of Chicago.[65]

1944: Maril's art is included in *Artists for Victory* exhibition, mounted by American Federation of Arts. The exhibition opens at the Metropolitan Museum of Art in New York and then travels around the United States.[66]

1944, January 7–10: Maril is granted leave from his army service at Newton D. Baker General Hospital, Martinsburg, West Virginia, to attend his one-man exhibition at the Whyte Gallery, Washington, D.C.[67] The exhibition is on view January 10–31, 1944.[68]

1945, March 25: Maril wins award in Army arts contest at Newton D. Baker General Hospital, Martinsburg, West Virginia, for his painting *Pieta of 1944*.[69]

1945, September 13: Maril is separated from the United States Army.[70]

1945, September: Maril works at the Phillips Collection for about ten days.[71]

1945–1946: Maril teaches at the King-Smith School and the Washington Workshop in Washington, D.C. He lives in Washington that year.[72]

1946, September: Maril begins teaching art at the University of Maryland part time.[73]

1946, September 22–October 20: Maril has one-man show at the Baltimore Museum of Art.[74]

1947: Maril begins teaching art full time at the University of Maryland.[75]

1947, January 3–31: Maril has one-man show at the Robert Carlen Gallery, Philadelphia, Pennsylvania.[76]

1948, February 16–March 6: Maril has one-man show at the Macbeth Gallery, New York.[77]

1948, June 8: Maril and Esta Cook are married.[78]

1948, Summer: Maril teaches classes in landscape painting at Camp Ritchie, Cascade, Maryland, offered by University of Maryland Art Department.[79]

1948, Summer: Maril and his wife honeymoon on Cape Cod, Massachusetts.[80]

1949, February: Maril has one-man show at Whyte Gallery, Washington, D.C.[81]

1950: Baltimore Museum of Art receives Cone sisters' bequest to them. Maril's art is included in this collection.[82]

1950: Herman Maril and Esta Maril's son David is born.[83]

1951, April: Maril has one-man show at the Macbeth Gallery, New York.[84]

1951, October 14–November: Maril has one-man show at Barnett Aden Gallery, Washington, D.C.[85]

1953, January 27–February 15: Maril has one-man show at Whyte Gallery, Washington, D.C.[86]

1953–Autumn to Spring 1954: Maril is guest instructor at Philadelphia Museum of Art.[87]

1953, November 2–21: Maril has one-man show at Babcock Gallery, New York.[88]

1954: Herman and Esta Maril's daughter Suzanne (now Nadja Maril Crilly) is born.[89]

1954–1960: Milton Avery visits Provincetown and is Maril's neighbor during the summers.[90]

1954, Autumn–Spring 1955: Maril is instructor at Philadelphia Museum of Art.[91]

1955: Maril has one-man show at the Philadelphia Art Alliance.[92]

1955, Autumn–Winter 1956: Maril teaches art at the Jewish Community Center, Baltimore.[93]

1956, March 26–April 14: Maril has one-man show at the Babcock Gallery in New York.[94]

1956, October: Maril has one-man show at the Franz Bader Gallery in Washington, D.C.[95]

1957, July 14: Maril painting *Inlet* is acquired by the Baltimore Museum of Art.[96]

1957, November 3–22: Maril has one-man show at the University of Maryland.[97]

1958, August: Maril is included in the First Annual Provincetown Arts Festival.[98]

1958: Mark Rothko buys house next to the Marils at Provincetown, Massachusetts.[99]

1958, Autumn: The Marils buy former post office to use as a home in Provincetown, Massachusetts.[100]

1959, March 9–28: Maril has one-man show at the Babcock Gallery in New York.[101]

1959: Maril builds a studio onto his Provincetown, Massachusetts, house.[102]

1960, February: Maril has one-man show at Franz Bader Gallery, Washington, D.C.[103]

1961, January 23–February 13: Maril has one-man show at the Castellane Gallery, New York.[104]

1961, April 18–May 21: Maril one-man show at the Corcoran Gallery of Art, Washington, D.C.[105]

1962, February 13–March 13: Maril has one-man show at the Castellane Gallery, New York.[106]

1962, April–May: Maril has one-man show at the Franz Bader Gallery, Washington, D.C.[107]

1962, December 11: Herman Maril writes to Richard Castellane, breaking off his connection with the Castellane Gallery.[108]

1962, Summer: Maril paints on Monhegan Island, Maine.[109]

1963: Maril's painting, *The Aviary*, wins the top award in the New England Exhibition of Painting and Sculpture, Silvermine Guild of Artists, New Canaan, Connecticut. The judge was Lloyd Goodrich, director of the Whitney Museum of American Art.[110]

1963: Maril's painting, *Sand and Water*, wins the top award in the Mead Painting of the Year Southeastern Exhibition, Atlanta, Georgia. The judges were Anthony Bower, manager-editor, *Art in America*; Charles P. Parkhurst Jr., Baltimore Museum of Art; and Henry Geldzahler, Metropolitan Museum of Art.[111]

1963, April 20–May 16: Maril has one-man show at the Athena Gallery, New Haven, Connecticut.[112]

1963, August 31: Bella Fishko of Forum Gallery writes to Herman Maril saying she would like to give him an exhibition.[113]

1963, December 6–31: Maril has one-man show at the Franz Bader Gallery, Washington, D.C.[114]

1964, August 2–13: Maril has exhibition of recent paintings at the Wellfleet Gallery, Cape Cod.[115]

1965, March 6–26: Maril has his first one-man show at the Forum Gallery, New York.[116]

1965, October 17–November 9: Maril has one-man show at Baltimore Junior College Fine Arts Center.[117]

1967: The Herman Maril family moves to house on Roxbury Place, in the Mount Washington neighborhood of Baltimore, Maryland. They previously lived nearby.[118]

1967, September: Maril has one-man show at Baltimore Museum of Art, accompanied by monographic book.[119] the exhibition and the book were dedicated to the memory of Dr. Mason Lord, a collector of art by Maril and other artists, and a pioneer in the field of geriatrics.[120]

1968, August 26–September 7: Maril has one-man show at Wellfleet Art Gallery, Cape Cod, Massachusetts.[121]

1968, January 27–February 16: Maril has one-man show at Forum Gallery, New York City, New York.[122]

1968, March 27–April 13: Maril has one-man show, Franz Bader Gallery, Washington, D.C.[123]

1969: Herman, Esta, and Suzanne Maril travel to Mexico.[124]

1969, December: Maril travels to Colorado and New Mexico to make paintings for Bureau of Reclamation. Maril completes the paintings in 1970.[125]

1970: Maril has one-man show at Wellfleet Art Gallery, Cape Cod, Massachusetts.[126]

1971, February 13–March 5: Maril has one-man show at Forum Gallery, New York.[127]

1972, March: Maril is included in exhibition of The American Artist and Water Reclamation at the National Gallery of Art, Washington, D.C.[128]

1972, March 28–April 15: Maril has one-man show at Franz Bader Gallery, Washington, D.C.[129]

1973, Summer: Maril travels to tapestry atelier in Paris to learn about the medium.[130]

1973, Summer: Herman and Esta Maril travel to Italy with friends Bill and Louise Rowles.[131]

1974, July 29–August 10: Maril has one-man show at Wellfleet Art Gallery, Cape Cod, Massachusetts.[132]

1974: The Marils travel to California.[133]

1974, March 30–April 15: Maril has one-man show of paintings and tapestries at the Forum Gallery, New York.[134]

1975: Maril's painting *Marsh Birds*, in collection of the Whitney Museum of American Art, is chosen to hang at

Admiralty House, the residence of Vice President Nelson Rockefeller.[135]

1975, October 22–November 8: Maril has one-man show at Franz Bader Gallery, Washington, D.C.[136]

1977, February 17–March 17: Maril has one-man show at the University of Maryland Art Gallery, College Park, Maryland.[137]

1977, Spring: Maril retires from teaching at the University of Maryland.[138]

1977, March 5–25: Maril has a one-man show at the Forum Gallery, New York.[139]

1978: Maril has one-man show at the American Institute of Arts and Letters, New York.[140]

1980, November 12–29: Maril has one-man show at the Franz Bader Gallery, Washington, D.C.[141]

1980, March 29–April 18: Maril has one-man show at the Forum Gallery, New York.[142]

1981: Maril has one-man show at the University of Virginia Art Museum, Charlottesville, Virginia.[143]

1983: Maril has one-man show at the Forum Gallery, New York.[144]

1983, Spring: Maril is hospitalized for two months, gravely ill.[145]

1984: Maril has one-man show at the Wichita Art Museum, Wichita, Kansas.[146]

1985: Herman and Esta Maril travel to Portugal and Spain.[147]

1984, April–May 13: Maril has one-man exhibition of works on paper at G. H. Dalsheimer Gallery, Baltimore, Maryland.[148]

1985, January 5: The University of Maryland presents an honorary doctorate of Fine Arts to Maril.[149]

1986, September 6: Herman Maril dies of pneumonia in Hyannis, Massachusetts.[150]

Notes

1 Frank Getlein, *Herman Maril* (Baltimore, MD: Baltimore Museum of Art, 1967), 19.

2 "Maryland Institute Head Is Named by Governors," *Baltimore Sun*, 14 July 1920, 20.

3 Phillips Collection and Eliza E. Rathbone, *Duncan Phillips Centennial Exhibition*. (Washington, D.C.: Phillips Collection, 1999), 30.

4 William Hauptman, "The Artist Speaks: An Interview between Herman Maril and William Hauptman," in *Herman Maril* (College Park, MD: University of Maryland Art Department Gallery, 1977), 17–20.

5 Getlein, *Herman Maril*, 19.

6 Howard E. Wooden, "Herman Maril: A Retrospective Exhibition of Paintings, 1926-1983," (Wichita Art Museum, March 26, 1984), 5–6.

7 Roger Eliot Fry, *Cézanne: A Study of His Development* (New York: Noonday Press, 1958).; Herman Maril, interview by Dorothy Seckler, July 5, 1965, Archives of American Art, Provincetown, Massachusetts, http://www.aaa.si.edu/collections/interviews/oral-history-interview-herman-maril-11701.

8 Duncan Phillips, *An Exhibition of Expressionist Painters from the Experiment Station of the Phillips Memorial Gallery* (Washington, D.C.: Phillips Memorial Gallery, 1927).; Duncan Phillips, *Catalogue of the Exhibition of American Themes by American Painters Lent by Phillips Memorial Gallery, Washington, D.C.* (Washington, D.C.: Phillips Memorial Gallery, 1927).

9 Getlein, *Herman Maril*, 19.

10 Ibid., 12.; Hauptman, "The Artist Speaks: An Interview between Herman Maril and William Hauptman," 20.

11 Herman Maril, "Speech for University College Commencement," typescript (Herman Maril Foundation, Baltimore, Maryland, 1985), Herman Maril Foundation.

12 "Independent Art Show Not Radical," *Baltimore Sun*, October 8, 1933, sec. SF.

13 Esta Maril, "The Two Worlds of Herman Maril," *Herman Maril: An Artist's Two Worlds* (Provincetown, MA: Provincetown Art Association and Museum, 2008).

14 B. W. Sweaney, "C. H. Walther Is Ousted by MD. Institute," *Baltimore Sun*, July 30, 1929.

15 Duncan Phillips, Erika D. Passantino, and David W. Scott, *The Eye of Duncan Phillips: A Collection in the Making* (Washington, D.C.: Phillips Collection in association with Yale University New Haven, 1999), 248–50.

16 National Society of Independent Artists, *Catalogue of the Second Exhibition 1933 of the National Society of Independent Artists* (Washington, D.C.: National Society of Independent Artists, 1933), 3, 9.

17 Phillips, Passantino, and Scott, *The Eye of Duncan Phillips*, 31.

18 "Baltimoreans in N. Y. Show," *Baltimore Sun*, December 10, 1933, sec. SA.; Museum of Modern Art, *Painting and Sculpture from 16 American Cities* (New York: The Museum of Modern Art, 1933).

19 Herman Maril, interview by Ronald Becker, Archives of American Art, July 22, 1981.

20 Edward B. Rowan, "Letter from Edward B. Rowan to Herman Maril Commending His Art Seen at Studio House and Saying He Is Glad Maril Had Been Hired on to PWAP," letter (January 23, 1934), Herman Maril Foundation.

21 Public Works of Art Project, "Class A Artist, Becker, Hermand [Sic] M., 3810 Park Heights Ave., Baltimore, MD," May 26, 1934, Baltimore Museum of Art Archives, Public Works of Art Project, Records for the State of Maryland.

22 Edward B. Rowan, "Letter from Edward B. Rowan to Herman Maril Saying His Sketch of Old Baltimore Water Front Had Arrived and Was Much Appreciated, letter (February 17, 1934), Herman Maril Foundation.

23 Forbes Watson, "A Steady Job," *American Magazine of Art*, April 1934, 179.

24 Herman Maril, "Letter from Herman Maril to Elmira Bier of the Phillips Memorial Gallery about Purchases of Art by Duncan Phillips," (December 11, 1934), Phillips Collection.

25 Public Works of Art Project, *National Exhibition of Art, by the Public Works of Art Project, April 24, 1934 to May 20, 1934 (Inclusive) the Corcoran Gallery of Art, Washington, District of Columbia* (Washington, D.C.: U. S. Government Printing Office, 1934).

26 "Paintings Chosen for White House," *Washington Star*, May 12, 1934.; "Art Is Viewed by First Lady," *Washington Post*, May 12, 1934, Herman Maril Foundation.

27 Malcolm Vaughan, "Modern Museum Exhibits Art Produced by New Deal," *New York American*, September 1934.; "PWAP Art Show Here: Exhibition to Be Opened at Modern Museum Wednesday," *New York Times*, September 16, 1934, sec. N.

28 Herman Maril, "Letter from Herman Maril to Elmira Bier of the Phillips Memorial Gallery about Purchases of Art by Duncan Phillips."; Phillips Collection, *The Phillips Collection: A Summary Catalogue* (Washington, D.C.: The Phillips Collection, 1985), 147.

29 "Exhibition of Paintings in Oil and Gouache by Herman Maril, 28th November - 21st December, Howard University Gallery of Art," 1934, Herman Maril Foundation.

30 "Last Week of Exhibit at Museum," *Baltimore Sun*, April 28, 1935, sec. SC, 11.

31 Olin Dows, "Herman Maril," *American Magazine of Art*, July 1935.

32 Herman Maril, interview by Dorothy Seckler.; Katherine Frazier, "Letter from Katherine Frazier Inviting Herman Maril to Teach at Cummington School for the Arts in 1936," letter (January 11, 1936), Herman Maril Foundation. Frazier's letter saying "I wonder if you want to come back to us. We would like to have you. I was glad to know that you felt it a fine experience and that the coordination was valuable." Therefore, clearly Maril had taught at Cummington in the summer of 1935. In his interview by Dorothy Seckler, Maril says that he taught at Cummington for six years. That was from 1935 to 1940.

33 Vylla Poe Wilson, "Fourteenth Biennial Exhibition Focuses Art World's Eyes on Corcoran Gallery Here," *Washington Post*, March 3, 1935, sec. SA, 5.

34 "Studio House Artists Show in Philadelphia," *ARTnews (U.S.A.)*, February 8, 1936, The Phillips Collection.

35 Gallery Manager (Adele Smith?), "Letter from Studio House to Herman Maril about April 1936 Group Show," letter (March 19, 1936), Phillips Collection.

36 Herman Maril, interview by Dorothy Seckler.; "Summer News of Art," *New York Sun*, August 15, 1936.; *The Cummington School, Cummington, Massachusetts, 1937* (Cummington, MA: Playhouse-in-the-Hills, 1937). "Summer News of Art" informs us, "The summer art exhibit at the Cummington School, Cummington, Mass., offers works by Chaim Gross, New York sculptor, and Herman Maril, painter and teacher of Baltimore, both of whom are instructors at the school in the Berkshires this summer." Cummington's 1937 yearbook includes a photograph of the young Herman Maril teaching as two students work at easels. It also lists Maril as among the 1936 faculty.

37 "A Reviewer's Notebook: Among New Exhibitions," *New York Times*, November 1, 1936, sec. X.; Olin Dows, *Paintings by Herman Maril* (New York: Marie Sterner Galleries, 1936).; Herman Maril, interview by Robert Brown, July 21, 1971.

38 Boyer Galleries, Inc., *Recent Paintings: Herman Maril* (Philadelphia, PA: Boyer Galleries, Inc., 1937).

39 Herman Maril, interview by Dorothy Seckler.; "Herman Maril's Work at Cummington School," *Springfield Union and Republican*, July 18, 1937, Herman Maril Foundation.

40 "C. H. Walther, Noted Artist, Dies of Injury," *Baltimore Sun*, May 8, 1938, 20.

41 Herman Maril, interview by Robert Brown.

42 Herman Maril, interview by Dorothy Seckler.; Sheldon Hurst, "Friendship," *Painter & Poet: The Art of Herman Maril, the Poems of William Bronk: A Collection of Letters* (Queensbury, NY: Adirondack Community College, 2008), 5.

43 "Works of Local Artists to Be Shown at Chicago," *Baltimore Sun*, October 14, 1938, 8.

44 A. D. Emmart, "Art - Herman Maril Exhibition at Baltimore Museum," *Baltimore Sun*, February 12, 1939.

45 Whyte Gallery, "Young Washington Paintings: Former 'Studio House' Exhibitors" (Whyte Gallery, 1939).; "Whyte Show Opens March 30," *Washington Post*, March 15, 1939.; Leslie Judd Portner, "Bader Opens a New Gallery," *Washington Post*, April 4 1954, sec. ST.

46 Getlein, *Herman Maril*, 21.; "Maryland Artists Recognized in Fair," *Baltimore Sun*, January 8, 1939, 3.

47 Getlein, *Herman Maril*, 21.

48 "Contract between the United States of America and Herman Maril, Artist," May 12, 1939, Herman Maril Foundation.

49 Herman Maril, interview by Dorothy Seckler.; Cummington School, *The Cummington School, Cummington, Massachusetts, 1940* (Cummington, MA:

49 Playhouse-in-the-Hills, 1940). Maril is listed on the faculty, reflecting his work there in 1939.

50 Leslie Judd Ahlander, "Show Marks Bader Anniversary," *Washington Post*, March 9, 1964.

51 Whyte Gallery, *Paintings by Herman Maril* (Washington, D.C.: Whyte Gallery, 1940).

52 Metropolitan Museum of Art, "Letter from the Metropolitan Museum of Art to Herman Maril Saying That Press Release Would Soon Be Going out Announcing the Purchase of Paintings Including Maril's In the Kitchen," letter (August 1, 1940), Herman Maril Foundation.

53 Herman Maril, interview by Dorothy Seckler.

54 Alfred D. Charles, "From Show Card Writing to Metropolitan Museum," *Baltimore Sun*, November 3, 1940, sec. M.

55 Edward B. Rowan, "Letter from Edward B. Rowan to Herman Maril about West Scranton Branch Post Office Mural," letter (January 28, 1941), Herman Maril Foundation. This letter says that Maril's contract is being prepared.

56 "Figures Prophetic of Herman Maril's Future," *Art Digest*, March 1941, Herman Maril Foundation.

57 Herman Maril-Donald Coale School of Painting, "Advertisement and Registrar Card for Herman Maril-Donald Coale School of Painting," 1941, Herman Maril Foundation.

58 Olin Dows, "Letter from Olin Dows to Herman Maril about Posters and Report for Office of Civilian Defense," letter (January 22, 1942), Herman Maril Foundation.

59 Metropolitan Museum of Art, *On the Bright Side: A Loan Exhibition of Contemporary American Painting & Sculpture* (New York, NY: Metropolitan Museum of Art, 1942).

60 Edward B. Rowan, "Letter from Edward B. Rowan to Herman Maril Saying His Work Has Won a Purchase Award in the O. E. M. Competition for Pictures to Record Defense and War Activities," letter (February 5, 1942), Herman Maril Foundation.

61 American Red Cross, "Pictures Purchased from the American Red Cross Competition to Record Its Numerous Activities Conducted by the Section of Fine Arts" (American Red Cross, April 12, 1942), Herman Maril Foundation.

62 Herman Maril, interview by Dorothy Seckler.

63 Macbeth Gallery, "Gouaches and Water Colors by Corp. Herman Maril, U.S. Army" (Macbeth Gallery, 1943).

64 Herman Maril, "The WPA Art Project," *Baltimore Evening Sun*, 25 June 1943.

65 "Maril's Painting at Chicago Show," *Baltimore Sun*, October 31, 1943, sec. M, 9.; Eleanor Jewett, "54th Show of U.S. Paintings Opens Oct. 27," *Chicago Daily Tribune*, October 17, 1943, sec. F, 6.

66 "Painting Selected for National Tour," *Baker's Batter: Newton D. Baker General Hospital*, November 15, 1944, 3.

67 Kermit E. Larson, "Leave Permission for Herman Maril to Visit Washington to Attend an Exhibition of His Paintings," letter (December 20, 1943), Herman Maril Foundation.

68 Whyte Gallery, "New Paintings by Herman Maril" (Whyte Gallery, 1944).

69 "Maryland Soldier Wins Art Award at Baker General," *Washington Post*, March 26, 1945.

70 "Army Separation Qualification Record Herman Maril," September 13, 1945, Herman Maril Foundation.

71 Herman Maril, interview by Dorothy Seckler.

72 Ibid.

73 "Two Teachers Added at University," *Baltimore Sun*, September 16, 1946, 15.

74 "3 Maryland Artists' Works to Be Exhibited," *Baltimore Sun*, September 18, 1946.

75 Getlein, *Herman Maril*, 20.

76 Robert Carlen Gallery, "Recent Paintings by Herman Maril" (Robert Carlen Gallery, 1947).

77 James Herring, *Herman Maril* (New York: Macbeth Gallery, 1948).

78 Maril, "The Two Worlds of Herman Maril."

79 "Summer Classes in Art Announced by U. of Md.," *Baltimore Sun*, April 19, 1948, 7.

80 Ibid.

81 Jane Watson Crane, "Conviction Is Byword for Maril," *Washington Post*, February 13, 1949, sec. L, 5.

82 Brenda Richardson, William C. Ameringer, and Baltimore Museum of Art, *Dr. Claribel & Miss Etta: The Cone Collection of the Baltimore Museum of Art* (Baltimore, MD: Baltimore Museum of Art, 1985), 9, 153.

83 Getlein, *Herman Maril*, 20.

84 Macbeth Galleries, *Herman Maril: Paintings* (New York: Macbeth Galleries, 1951).

85 Herman Maril, interview by Dorothy Seckler.

86 D. R. K., "Whyte's Showing Maril Work," *Washington Post*, February 1, 1953, sec. L, 5.

87 Herman Maril, interview by Dorothy Seckler.

88 Babcock Galleries, *Herman Maril: Recent Paintings, November 2 - 21, 1953* (New York, NY: Babcock Galleries, 1953).

89 Getlein, *Herman Maril*, 20.

90 Louis Newman, "Cross Currents," *Cross Currents: Milton Avery, Karl Knaths, Herman Maril* (New York, NY: David Findlay Jr. Fine Art, 2007), 2.

91 Herman Maril, interview by Dorothy Seckler.

92 Getlein, *Herman Maril*, 20.

93 "Art Instructors Named for Jewish Course," *Baltimore Sun*, October 9, 1955.

94 Babcock Galleries, *Herman Maril* (New York, NY: Babcock Galleries, 1956).

95 Portner, "Bader Opens a New Gallery."

96 Kenneth B. Sawyer, "Guggenheim, Baltimore Acquisitions," *Baltimore Sun*, July 14, 1957, sec. F.

97 "Exhibition by Maril Slated Next Month," *Baltimore Sun*, October 23, 1957, 23.

98 Kenneth B. Sawyer, "'Sad Shake of Head' over Art Festival," *Baltimore Sun*, August 17, 1958, sec. F.

99 David Maril, interview by Ann Prentice Wagner, March 31, 2010.

100 David Maril to Ann Prentice Wagner, "Herman Maril Biographical Information," January 9, 2016.

101 Babcock Galleries, *Herman Maril* (New York, NY: Babcock Galleries, 1959).

102 Maril to Wagner, "Herman Maril Biographical Information."

103 Kenneth B. Sawyer, "A Place of Mystery and Beauty," *Baltimore Sun*, February 7, 1960, sec. A, 16.

104 Castellane Gallery, "Herman Maril" (Castellane Gallery, 1961).; "N. Y. Gallery Sets Maril Art Exhibit," *Baltimore Evening Sun*, January 27, 1961.

105 Kenneth B. Sawyer, "Maril Exhibition in Capital," *Baltimore Sun*, April 30, 1961, sec. A, 2.

106 Castellane Gallery, "Recent Paintings of Herman Maril" (Castellane Gallery, 1962).; S. T., "Herman Maril," *Arts Magazine*, April 1962, 57.

107 "Capital Area Art Activities," *Washington Post*, April 22, 1962, sec. G.; L. J. A., "Maril Shows Intensity," *Washington Post*, May 6, 1962, sec. G.

108 Herman Maril, "Letter from Herman Maril to Richard Castellane," letter (December 11, 1962), Herman Maril Foundation.

109 Getlein, *Herman Maril*, 20.

110 Margaret Harold, *Prize-Winning Paintings: Representational and Abstract* (Ford Lauderdale, FL: Allied Publications, Inc., 1964), R-32.

111 Ibid., R-33.

112 Athena Gallery, "Invitation to an Exhibition of the Paintings of Herman Maril, April 20 - May 16, 1963, the Athena Gallery," (Athena Gallery, 1963).

113 Bella Fishko, "Letter from Bella Fishko of Forum Gallery to Herman Maril," letter (August 31, 1963), Herman Maril Foundation.

114 Franz Bader Gallery, "Herman Maril" (Franz Bader Gallery, 1963).

115 Kenneth B. Sawyer, *Herman Maril: Recent Paintings* (Cape Cod, MA: Wellfleet Art Gallery, 1964).

116 Forum Gallery, *Herman Maril* (New York, NY: Forum Gallery, 1965).

117 Bennard B. Perlman, *Herman Maril: Inaugural Exhibition, Baltimore Junior College* (Baltimore, MD: Baltimore Junior College, 1965).; Cherrill Anson, "Finally, Home Is the Artist," *Baltimore Sun*, October 24, 1965, sec. D, 26.

118 Maril to Wagner, "Herman Maril Biographical Information."

119 Getlein, *Herman Maril*.

120 "'Pleased . . . by the Forms of Nature': Maril Exhibition to Honor Dr. Lord," *Baltimore Sun*, September 9, 1967, sec. A, 8.; Barbara Gold, "Herman Maril Retrospective," *Baltimore Sun*, September 17, 1967, sec. F, 4.

121 "One-Man Exhibition," *Baltimore Sun*, August 22, 1968, sec. B, 6.

122 Forum Gallery, *Herman Maril* (New York, New York: Forum Gallery, 1968).

123 Franz Bader Gallery, "Herman Maril" (Franz Bader Gallery, 1968).; Paul Richard, "Paintings at the Corcoran Cause Hostility by Viewers," *Washington Post*, March 31, 1968, sec. G, 9.

124 Nadja Maril, interview by Ann Prentice Wagner, June 19, 2011.

125 "Slightly Different Dunes: But Local Artists Still Out to Paint," *Provincetown Advocate*, December 4, 1969.; Gary Vikan, "Forward," *Herman Maril: An Artist's Two Worlds* (Provincetown, MA: The Provincetown Art Association and Museum, 2008).

126 Herman. Maril et al., *Herman Maril: An Artist's Two Worlds* (Provincetown, MA: Provincetown Art Association and Museum, 2008).

127 Forum Gallery, "Invitation to the Preview of an Exhibition of Recent Paintings by Herman Maril, February 13 - March 5, 1971, Forum Gallery" (Forum Gallery, 1971).; Frank Getlein, "Herman Maril's Serene Unity," *Evening Star*, March 4, 1971, sec. C, 6.

128 National Gallery of Art, "Invitation to Exhibition Preview for the American Artist and Water Reclamation, National Gallery of Art" (National Gallery of Art, 1972).

129 Franz Bader Gallery, "Invitation to Preview of Herman Maril: An Exhibition of His Recent Works, at Franz Bader Gallery, Tuesday, March 28, 1972" (Franz Bader Gallery, 1972).

130 Herman Maril, "Letter to George Levitine about Tapestries," letter (January 16, 1975).

131 Louise Rowles and Bill Rowles, interview by Ann Prentice Wagner, April 27, 2010.

132 Wellfleet Art Gallery, "Invitation to Exhibition of Herman Maril Paintings, Abbott Pattison Sculpture, Wellfleet Art Gallery, July 29 - August 10, 1974" (Wellfleet Art Gallery, 1974).

133 University of Maryland, University College, *His Own Path: The Spirit and Legacy of Herman Maril*, 35.

134 Forum Gallery, *Herman Maril: Paintings and Tapestries, March 30 to April 15, 1974* (New York, NY: Forum Gallery, 1974).; "Maril Exhibit Opens in N. Y.," *Baltimore Sun*, March 31, 1974, sec. D, 17.

135 Christian Renninger, "Herman Maril: Hanging around Admiralty House," *Precis*, November 7, 1975.

136 Franz Bader Gallery, "Invitation to Herman Maril: Selected Paintings, October 22 - November 8, 1975, Franz Bader Gallery," (Franz Bader Gallery, 1975).; Benjamin Forgey, "At the Galleries," *Washington Star*, October 31, 1975, sec. C, 2.

137 "Public Occurrences," *Washington Post*, February 17, 1977, sec. MD, 14.; Lincoln F. Johnson, "The Joys of Maril's Exhibit," *Baltimore Sun*, March 3,1977.

138 George Levitine, "Letter from George Levitine to Herman Maril Acknowledging His Request to Retire from Teaching at the University of Maryland," letter (April 19, 1977), Herman Maril Foundation.; David Maril, interview by Ann Prentice Wagner, May 20, 2016.Business, (19 April 1977

139 Forum Gallery, "Invitation to the Opening of an Exhibition of Recent Paintings by Herman Maril, March 5, 1977 - March 25, 1977, Forum Gallery," (Forum Gallery, 1977).

140 Maril et al., *Herman Maril*.

141 Franz Bader Gallery & Bookstore, "Invitation to Herman Maril: Paintings, Drawings, Prints, November 12 - 29, 1980, Franz Bader Gallery & Bookstore" (Franz Bader Gallery & Bookstore, 1980).; Benjamin Forgey, "Maril: An Interior Vision, a Strong Note of Reverie," *Washington Star*, November 28, 1980.

142 Forum Gallery, "Invitation to an Exhibition of Recent Paintings by Herman Maril, March 29 - April 18, 1980, Forum Gallery," (Forum Gallery, 1980).

143 Gladys Blizzard, *Works by Herman Maril from Charlottesville Collectors* (Charlottesville, VA: University of Virginia Art Museum, 1981).

144 Forum Gallery, "Invitation to an Exhibition of Recent Paintings by Herman Maril, March 5 - March 26, 1983, Forum Gallery" (Forum Gallery, 1983).

145 Elsa A. Solender, "Visions Rich & Simple: Painter Herman Maril Has Spent a Lifetime Paring Down a Complex Vision of the Bare Essentials," *Messenger*, April 11, 1984, 10.

146 Wooden, "Herman Maril: A Retrospective Exhibition of Paintings, 1926-1983."

147 David Maril, "E-mail to Ann Prentice Wagner with Answers to Maril Biographical Questions," email January 7, 2016.

148 John Dorsey, "In a Blatant Age, Maril's Art Is Quiet and Subtle," *Baltimore Sun*, April 15, 1984, sec. L, 8.

149 University of Maryland, University College, "Herman Maril Honorary Degree of Doctor of Fine Arts, University of Maryland, University College, January 5, 1985" (University of Maryland, University College, January 5, 1985), Phillips Collection.

150 "Herman Maril Is Dead at 77; Landscape Artist and Teacher," *New York Times*, September 12, 1986, sec. D, 20.

BIBLIOGRAPHY

"3 Maryland Artists' Works to Be Exhibited." *Baltimore Sun*. September 18, 1946.

"1930 United States Federal Census," 1930.

A., L. J. "Maril Shows Intensity." *Washington Post*. May 6, 1962, sec. G.

"A Reviewer's Notebook: Among New Exhibitions." *New York Times*. November 1, 1936, sec. X.

A Stately Heritage. Adelphi, Maryland: University of Maryland University College, 2000.

"About Town." *Where to Go in Baltimore*, July 10, 1042. Herman Maril Foundation.

"Accession Records for Works by Charles H. Walther into the Phillips Collection, Washington, D.C.," Beginning 1927. The Phillips Collection.

A.D.E. "Exhibition by Modernists." *The Baltimore Sun*. January 16, 1926.

———. "Exhibitions of Paintings." *The Baltimore Sun*. March 24, 1926.

———. "Further Views on All-City Show at Baltimore Museum." *The Baltimore Sun*. April 11, 1926.

"Advises Modernist Art Group Disband." *The Baltimore Sun*. October 24, 1926.

Ahlander, Leslie Judd. "Show Marks Bader Anniversary." *Washington Post*. March 9, 1964.

"All-Baltimore Show Jurors to Start Work." *The Baltimore Sun*. March 21, 1926.

American Red Cross. "Pictures Purchased from the American Red Cross Competition to Record Its Numerous Activities Conducted by the Section of Fine Arts." American Red Cross, April 12, 1942. Herman Maril Foundation.

Anson, Cherrill. "Finally, Home Is the Artist." *Baltimore Sun*. October 24, 1965, sec. D.

Archives of American Art. "American Arts Group Records, 1934-1965." *American Artists Group Records, 1934-1965*. Accessed August 29, 2015. http://www.aaa.si.edu/collections/american-artists-group-records-6979.

Argersinger, Jo Ann E. "The City That Tries to Suit Everybody: Baltimore's Clothing Industry." In *The Baltimore Book: New Views of Local History*, 80–101. Philadelphia: Temple University Press, 1991.

"Army Separation Qualification Record Herman Maril," September 13, 1945. Herman Maril Foundation.

"Art Instructors Named for Jewish Course." *Baltimore Sun*. October 9, 1955.

"Art Is Viewed by First Lady." *Washington Post*. May 12, 1934. Herman Maril Foundation.

"Art Notes." *Washington Post*. October 14, 1951, sec. L.

"Artist Once Hoped to Become Engineer." *The Baltimore Evening Sun*. October 24, 1947.

Ashton, Dore. "Art: 106 casein painters." *New York Times*. March 13, 1959.

Athena Gallery. "Invitation to an Exhibition of the Paintings of Herman Maril, April 20 - May 16, 1963, the Athena Gallery." Athena Gallery, 1963.

Babcock Galleries. *Herman Maril*. New York, New York: Babcock Galleries, 1956.

———. *Herman Maril*. New York, New York: Babcock Galleries, 1959.

———. *Herman Maril: Recent Paintings, November 2 - 21, 1953*. New York, New York: Babcock Galleries, 1953.

Baer, Susan. "Herman Maril - Developing and Working." *Baltimore Sun Magazine*, March 5, 1983.

Balder, Alton Parker. *Six Maryland Artists*. Baltimore, MD: Balboa Publications, 1955.

Ball, Charlotte, ed. *Who's Who in American Art: Herman Maril*. Vol. 3. Washington, D.C.: The American Federation of Arts, 1940.

"Baltimoreans in N. Y. Show." *Baltimore Sun*. December 10, 1933, sec. SA.

Baltimore Polytechnic Institute. "Web Site Baltimore Polytechnic Institute." *Baltimore Polytechnic Institute Web Site*. Accessed February 15, 2015. http://www.bpi.edu/history.jsp/.

Barr, Pamela T., ed. *The Tides of Provincetown: Pivotal Years in America's Oldest Continuous Art Colony (1899-2011)*. Lebanon, N.H.: University Press of New England, 2011.

Barr, Jr., Alfred H. *Cubism and Abstract Art*. New York: The Museum of Modern Art, 1936.

"Beach at Chatham, by Aaron Sopher." *Baltimore Sun*. November 11, 1934, sec. SA.

Becker, Ronald. Interview with Ronald Becker by Ann Prentice Wagner at Mount Washington house. Interview by Ann Prentice Wagner. Oral interview, June 16, 2010. Herman Maril Foundation.

———. Phone interview at David Maril's Mount Washington House. Interview by Ann Prentice Wagner. Telephone interview, May 20, 2013.

Bement, Alon. *The Energetic Line in Figure Drawing*. Mineola, New York: Dover Publications, Inc., 2009.

Bier, Elmira. Business. "Letter from Elmira Bier of the Phillips Collection to Herman Maril about the Purchase of Two Paintings by Duncan Phillips." Business, December 10, 1934. Herman Maril Foundation.

Bishop, Audrey. "At Home with Herman Maril, Unofficial Dean of Maryland Painters." *The News American*. October 12, 1980, sec. C.

Blizzard, Gladys. *Works by Herman Maril from Charlottesville Collectors*. Charlottesville, Virginia: University of Virginia Art Museum, 1981.

Bosworth, Patricia. *Diane Arbus: A Biography*. New York: Alfred A. Knopf, 1984.

Boyer Galleries, Inc. *Recent Paintings: Herman Maril*. Philadelphia, Pennsylvania: Boyer Galleries, Inc., 1937.

Breeskin, Adelyn D. Business. "Letter from Adelyn D. Breeskin to Mr. Hoen about Herman Maril." Business, 1936. Herman Maril Foundation.

"Breeskin, Adelyn Dohme, Nee Dohme." *Dictionary of Art Historians*. https://dictionaryofarthistorians.org/index.htm: The Department of Art, Art History, and Visual Studies, Duke University, 2015.

Breslin, James. *Mark Rothko: A Biography*. Chicago: The University of Chicago Press, 1993.

Bronk, William. "Untitled tribute to Herman Maril." In *Herman Maril*, 7. College Park, Maryland: University of Maryland Art Department Gallery, 1977.

"Bronze Medal Awarded to Landscape Painted by Marjorie Meurer." *Washington Post*. December 24, 1933, sec. SM.

Bruce, Edward. "Public Works of Art Project, Address of Edward Bruce, Secretary to the Advisory Committee to the Treasury on Fine Arts." Congressional Record, 1934. Baltimore Museum of Art Archives, Public Works of Art Project, Records for the State of Maryland.

Bruce, Edward. Government. "To the Artists." Government, June 28, 1934. Baltimore Museum of Art Archives, Public Works of Art Project, Records for the State of Maryland.

"C. H. Walther, Noted Artist, Dies of Injury." *The Baltimore Sun*. May 8, 1938.

Cambell, Helen H. Business. "Letter from Helen H. Cambell of the American Federation of Arts to Herman Maril." Business, June 13, 1935. Herman Maril Foundation.

"Capital Area Art Activities." *Washington Post*. April 22, 1962, sec. G.

Castellane Gallery. "Herman Maril." Castellane Gallery, 1961.

———. "Recent Paintings of Herman Maril." Castellane Gallery, 1962.

Cézanne, Paul, Gail Stavitsky, Katherine. Rothkopf, Ellen Handy, Montclair Art Museum., and Baltimore Museum of Art. *Cézanne and American Modernism*. [Montclair, N.J.]; [Baltimore, Md.]; New Haven [Conn.]: Montclair Art Museum; Baltimore Museum of Art; Yale University Press, 2009.

Charles, Alfred D. "From Show Card Writing to Metropolitan Museum." *Baltimore Sun*. November 3, 1940, sec. M.

Cheney, Sheldon. *The Story of Modern Art*. Rev. and enl. mid-Century ed. New York: Viking Press, 1958.

Cheney, Sheldon. *A Primer of Modern Art*. New York: Liveright Publishing Corporation, 1966.

Cohen, Jean Lawlor. *Washington Art Matters: Art Life in the Capital 1940-1990*. Washington, D.C.: Washington Arts Museum, 2013.

Cone, Etta. Letter. "Letter from Etta Cone to Herman Maril." Letter, January 20, 1942. Herman Maril Foundation.

———. Letter. "Letter from Etta Cone to Herman Maril." Letter, June 11, 1948. Herman Maril Foundation.

"Contract between the United States of America and Herman Maril, Artist," May 12, 1939. Herman Maril Foundation.

Corcoran Gallery of Art. *Corcoran Gallery of Art: American Paintings to 1945*. Edited by Sarah Cash, Emily Dana Shapiro, Lisa Maria Strong, and Jennifer Carson. Washington, DC: Manchester, VT: Corcoran Gallery of Art; in association with Hudson Hills Press, 2011.

Crane, Jane Watson. "Conviction Is Byword for Maril." *Washington Post*. February 13, 1949, sec. L.

———. "Paintings at the Whyte Gallery: Conviction Is Byword for Maril." *Washington Post*. February 13, 1949, sec. L.

"Cross Currents: Milton Avery, Karl Knaths, Herman Maril." David Findlay Jr. Fine Art, January 6, 2007.

Cummington School. *The Cummington School, Cummington, Massachusetts, 1940*. Cummington, Massachusetts: Playhouse-in-the-Hills, 1940.

David Findlay Jr. Gallery. *Herman Maril (1908 - 1986)*. New York: David Findlay Jr Gallery, 2013.

Dorsey, John. "Herman Maril: Baltimore Artist Captured Both the Linear and the Lyric." *Baltimore Sun*. September 9, 1986, sec. C.

———. "In a Blatant Age, Maril's Art Is Quiet and Subtle." *Baltimore Sun*. April 15, 1984, sec. L.

Dows, Olin. "Herman Maril." *The American Magazine of Art*, July 1935.

———. Business. "Letter from Olin Dows to Herman Maril about Posters and Report for Office of Civilian Defense." Business, January 22, 1942. Herman Maril Foundation.

———. *Paintings by Herman Maril*. New York: Marie Sterner Galleries, 1936.

"Druid Hill Park." *Department of Recreation and Parks*. Accessed August 6, 2015. http://bcrp.baltimorecity.gov/ParksTrails/DruidHillPark.aspx.

Edwards, Kathleen A., ed. *New Forms: The Avant-Garde Meets the American Scene, 1934-1949*. Iowa City, Iowa: University of Iowa Press, 2013.

"Eleanor Spencer, 97, Medieval-Art Scholar." *New York Times*. November 19, 1992.

Emmart, A. D. "Art - Works of the Baltimore Artists Union." *Baltimore Sun*. January 17, 1937, sec. SA.

———. "Art- Herman Maril Exhibition at Baltimore Museum." *Baltimore Sun*. February 12, 1939.

Etta, Cone. "Letters from Herman Maril Foundation," June 11, 1948. Baltimore, Maryland.

Everson Museum of Art, and Provincetown Art Association. *Provincetown Painters, 1890's-1970's*. Edited by Ronald A. Kuchta and Dorothy Gees Seckler. [Syracuse, N.Y: Visual Arts Publications, 1977.

"Exhibition by Maril Slated Next Month." *Baltimore Sun*. October 23, 1957.

"Exhibition of Paintings in Oil and Gouache by Herman Maril, 28th November - 21st December, Howard University Gallery of Art," 1934. Herman Maril Foundation.

F., H. K. "Shackelford Canvas Said to Take Honors in All-City Show." *Baltimore Sun*. March 28, 1926, sec. MT.

Falk, Peter Hastings. "Charles H. Walther." In *Who Was Who in American Art, 1564-1975: 400 Years of Artists in America*, 3455. II: P-Z. Madison, CT: Sound View Press, 1999.

———. "Hans Schuler." In *Who Was Who in American Art, 1564-1975: 400 Years of Artists in America*, 2941. II: P-Z. Madison, CT: Sound View Press, 1999.

———. "Herman Albert Becker." In *Who Was Who in American Art, 1564 - 1975: 400 Years of Artists in America*, 1: A-F:257. Madison, CT: Sound View Press, 1999.

———. "Shelby Shackelford." In *Who Was Who in American Art, 1564-1975: 400 Years of Artists in America*, 2983. II: P-Z. Madison, CT: Sound View Press, 1999.

"Figures Prophetic of Herman Maril's Future." *Art Digest*, March 1941. Herman Maril Foundation.

Fishko, Bella. Business. "Letter from Bella Fishko of Forum Gallery to Herman Maril." Business, August 31, 1963. Herman Maril Foundation.

Flam, Jack., Henri Matisse, Baltimore Museum of Art., Cone Collection., and Baltimore Museum of Art. *Matisse in the Cone Collection: The Poetics of Vision; Publ. on the Occasion of the Reopening of the Cone Collection, April 22, 2001.* Baltimore, Md.: Baltimore Museum of Art, 2001.

Fleming, Arlington. "City's Art Season Drives to a Close with Annual Print Show." *The Baltimore Sun*. May 1, 1927.

Fleming, H. Kingston. "Part of Philips Collection on View." *The Baltimore Sun*. April 17, 1927.

Forgey, Benjamin. "At the Galleries." *Washington Star*. October 31, 1975, sec. C.

———. "Maril: An Interior Vision, a Strong Note of Reverie." *Washington Star*. November 28, 1980.

Forum Gallery. *Herman Maril*. New York, New York: Forum Gallery, 1965.

———. *Herman Maril*. New York, New York: Forum Gallery, 1968.

———. *Herman Maril: Paintings and Tapestries, March 30 to April 15, 1974*. New York, New York: Forum Gallery, 1974.

———. "Invitation to an Exhibition of Recent Paintings by Herman Maril, March 5 - March 26, 1983, Forum Gallery." Forum Gallery, 1983.

———. "Invitation to an Exhibition of Recent Paintings by Herman Maril, March 29 - April 18, 1980, Forum Gallery." Forum Gallery, 1980.

———. "Invitation to the Opening of an Exhibition of Recent Paintings by Herman Maril, March 5, 1977 - March 25, 1977, Forum Gallery." Forum Gallery, 1977.

———. "Invitation to the Preview of an Exhibition of Recent Paintings by Herman Maril, February 13 - March 5, 1971, Forum Gallery." Forum Gallery, 1971.

Franz Bader Gallery. "Herman Maril." Franz Bader Gallery, 1963.

———. "Herman Maril." Franz Bader Gallery, 1968.

———. "Invitation to Herman Maril: Selected Paintings, October 22 - November 8, 1975, Franz Bader Gallery." Franz Bader Gallery, 1975.

———. "Invitation to Preview of Herman Maril: An Exhibition of His Recent Works, at Franz Bader Gallery, Tuesday, March 28, 1972." Franz Bader Gallery, 1972.

Franz Bader Gallery & Bookstore. "Invitation to Herman Maril: Paintings, Drawings, Prints, November 12 - 29, 1980, Franz Bader Gallery & Bookstore." Franz Bader Gallery & Bookstore, 1980.

Frazier, Katherine. Business. "Letter from Katherine Frazier Inviting Herman Maril to Teach at Cummington School for the Arts in 1936." Business, January 11, 1936. Herman Maril Foundation.

Frost, Douglas L., and College of Art. Maryland Institute. *MICA: Making History, Making Art*. Baltimore, MD: Maryland Institute College of Art, 2010.

Fry, Roger Eliot. *Cézanne: A Study of His Development*. Second. New York: Noonday Press, 1958.

G., A. "Herman Maril, Harold H. Wrenn Have 1-Man Shows in Baltimore." *Washington Post*. February 12, 1939, sec. L.

Gales, Gloria. "Manfred Schwartz Art 949-715-0308." *Manfred Schwartz, Master Colorist, Modern Artist (1909-1970)*. Accessed August 29, 2015. hattp://www.manfredschwartz.com/resume.html.

Gallery Manager (Adele Smith?). Business. "Letter from Studio House to Herman Maril about April 1936 Group Show." Business, March 19, 1936. Phillips Collection.

Gates, Margaret Casey. Business. "Letter from Studio House to Herman Maril about Paintings." Business, December 13, 1933. Herman Maril Foundation.

Getlein, Frank. *Herman Maril*. Baltimore, MD: Baltimore Museum of Art, 1967.

———."Herman Maril's Serene Unity." *The Evening Star*. March 4, 1971, sec. C.

Gilmore, Lyman. *The Force of Desire: A Life of William Bronk*. Jersey City, New Jersey: Talisman House, 2006.

Gold, Barbara. "Herman Maril Retrospective." *Baltimore Sun*. September 17, 1967, sec. F.

Graeme, Alice. "Whyte Gallery Shows Work by Local Group of 'Studio' Artists." *Washington Post*. December 3, 1939. Herman Maril Foundation.

Greif, Irvin. Interview at Baltimore home. Interview by Ann Prentice Wagner. In person interview, April 5, 2010.

Grieve, Victoria. *The Federal Art Project and the Creation of Middlebrow Culture*. Urbana: University of Illinois Press, 2009.

Grossman, Emery. *Art and Tradition*. New York: T. Yoseloff, 1968.

Harold, Margaret. *Prize-Winning Paintings: Representational and Abstract*. Ford Lauderdale, Florida: Allied Publications, Inc., 1964.

Harvey, Bill. "Hampden-Woodberry: Baltimore's Mill Villages." In *The Baltimore Book: New Views of Local History*, 38–55. Philadelphia: Temple University Press, 1991.

Hauptman, William. *Herman Maril*. College Park, Maryland: University of Maryland Art Department Gallery, 1977.

———. "The Artist Speaks: An Interview between Herman Maril and William Hauptman." In *Herman Maril*, 17–32. College Park, Maryland: University of Maryland Art Department Gallery, 1977.

Hayes, Bartlett, Richard J. Whalen, and Nina N. Kaiden, eds. *Artist and Advocate: An Essay on Corporate Patronage*. New York: Renaissance Editions, 1967.

Henry, Helen. "History by Lithography." *The Baltimore Sun*. May 4, 1969, sec. SM.

Herman Maril. Baltimore, Maryland: Axis Video, 1981.

"Herman Maril." Harmon-Meek Gallery, Naples, Florida, April 25, 1990.

"Herman Maril." David Findlay Jr. Fine Art, February 4, 2010.

"Herman Maril | Write On, Annapolis." Accessed August 6, 2015. https://nadjamaril.wordpress.com/tag/herman-maril/.

"Herman Maril, 77; Teacher, Artist; Noted for Cape Cod Landscapes." *Boston Globe*. September 13, 1986, Third Edition.

"Herman Maril: A Sense of Place." David Findlay Jr. Gallery, November 5, 2011.

"Herman Maril: A Survey of Paintings from the 1930s to the 1980s." David Findlay Jr. Fine Art, June 4, 2005.

"Herman Maril Is Dead at 77; Landscape Artist and Teacher." *New York Times*. September 12, 1986, sec. D.

"Herman Maril: Paintings." The Hyde Collection, Glens Falls, NY, July 18, 1991.

"Herman Maril: Paintings and Works on Paper from the 1920s and 1930s." James Graham and Sons Inc., June 29, 1999.

"Herman Maril: Search for the Essence." Mitchell Art Gallery, St. John's College, Annapolis, Maryland, 1995.

"Herman Maril: Seascapes." Academy of the Arts, Easton, Maryland, March 25, 1991.

"Herman Maril: The Early Years." Acme Fine Art and Design, November 14, 2004.

Herman Maril-Donald Coale School of Painting. "Advertisement and Registrar Card for Herman Maril-Donald Coale School of Painting," 1941. Herman Maril Foundation.

"Herman Maril's Work at Cummington School." *The Springfield Union and Republican*. July 18, 1937. Herman Maril Foundation.

Herring, James. *Herman Maril*. New York: Macbeth Gallery, 1948.

Hirschland, Ellen B., and Nancy H. Ramage. *The Cone Sisters of Baltimore: Collecting at Full Tilt*. Evanston, Ill.: Northwestern University Press, 2008.

H.K.F. "Modern Group Preparing for First Exhibit." *The Baltimore Sun*. January 17, 1926.

"Howard Exhibits Kuan-Yin Statue." *Washington Post*. November 12, 1934.

"Howard to Show African Culture." *Washington Post*. February 16, 1930.

"Howard University Gallery of Art: About Us." *History of the Gallery*, August 29, 2015. http://www.galleryofart.howard.edu/about-us/.

Hurst, Sheldon. "Friendship." In *Painter & Poet: The Art of Herman Maril, the Poems of William Bronk: A Collection of Letters*, 5–7. Queensbury, New York: Adirondack Community College, 2008.

"Independent Art Show Not Radical." *Baltimore Sun*. October 8, 1933, sec. SF.

"Independent Artists' Exhibition Draws Crowd, Baffling Many." *Baltimore Sun*. March 26, 1929.

"Independent Artists Name Their Officers." *Baltimore Sun*. May 13, 1928, sec. TM.

"Interior with Opening: Herman Maril Inside Looking Out." Galerie Francoise et ses freres, May 31, 2000.

Jacques, Kelly. "Esta Maril: The Longtime Park School Social Work Consultant Acted as Curator of Her Husband's Artwork, Archives." *Baltimore Sun*. April 26, 2009, sec. A.

Jensen, Peter. "Herman Maril, Baltimore Artist, Dies at Age 77." *Baltimore Sun*. September 8, 1986, sec. D.

Jewett, Eleanor. "54th Show of U.S. Paintings Opens Oct. 27." *Chicago Daily Tribune*. October 17, 1943, sec. F.

Johnson, Lincoln F. "The Joys of Maril's Exhibit." *The Baltimore Sun*. March 3, 1977.

Jury on Local Art, Baltimore Museum of Art. "Report of the Jury on Local Art to the Administrative Committee." Baltimore, Maryland: Baltimore Museum of Art, October 17, 1938. Herman Maril Foundation.

K, D R. "Whyte's Showing Maril Work." *Washington Post*. February 1, 1953, sec. L.

Kirkley, Donald. "Group Psychotherapy for Nervously Ill GIs." *Baltimore Sun*. December 30, 1945, sec. A.

Klank, Richard. Interview of Richard Klank by Ann Prentice Wagner at Herman Maril Foundation, Baltimore, Maryland. In person interview, April 12, 2010.

Krahulik, Karen Christel. *Provincetown: From Pilgrim Landing to Gay Resort*. New York and London: New York University Press, 2005.

Lanker, Brian, and Nicole Newnham. *They Drew Fire: Combat Artists of World War II*. New York: Brian Lanker Lanker Inc., 2000.

Larson, Kermit E. Business. "Leave Permission for Herman Maril to Visit Washington to Attend an Exhibition of His Paintings." Business, December 20, 1943. Herman Maril Foundation.

"Last Week of Exhibit at Museum." *Baltimore Sun*. April 28, 1935, sec. SC.

Lawless, Debra. *Provincetown: A History of Artists and Renegades in a Fishing Village*. Charleston, SC: History Press, 2011.

Lawton, Thomas. *Freer: A Legacy of Art*. Washington, D.C.: New York: Freer Gallery of Art, Smithsonian Institution; in association with H.N. Abrams, 1993.

Lee, Mordecai. *Promoting the War Effort Robert Horton and Federal Propaganda, 1938-1946.* Baton Rouge: Louisiana State University Press, 2012. http://site.ebrary.com/id/10603437.

Levitine, George. Business. "Letter from George Levitine to Herman Maril Acknowledging His Request to Retire from Teaching at the University of Maryland." Business, April 19, 1977. Herman Maril Foundation.

Longwell, Alicia G. "John Graham and the Quest for an American Art in the 1920s and 1930s." City University of New York, 2007.

Lopez-Remiro, Miguel, ed. *Writings on Art: Mark Rothko.* New Haven: Yale University Press, 2006.

Macbeth Galleries. *Herman Maril: Paintings.* New York: Macbeth Galleries, 1951.

Macbeth Gallery. "Gouaches and Water Colors by Corp. Herman Maril, U.S. Army." Macbeth Gallery, 1943.

"Manfred Schwartz, 60, Is Dead; Noted Painter and Lithographer." *New York Times.* November 8, 1970.

Marie Sterner Galleries. Business. "Letter from Marie Sterner Galleries to Herman Maril about Sales of Gouaches." Business, 1936. Herman Maril Foundation.

———. Business. "Letter from Marie Sterner Gallery with Statement of Account to Herman Maril." Business, November 25, 1936. Herman Maril Foundation.

Maril, David. "Baltimore Polytechnic Institute," February 15, 2015.

———. "E-mail to Ann Prentice Wagner with answers to Maril biographical questions," January 7, 2016.

———. Letter to Ann Prentice Wagner. "Herman Maril Biographical Information," January 9, 2016.

———. Interview with David Maril by Ann Prentice Wagner at Baltimore, Maryland. In person interview, February 15, 2011.

———. Interview with David Maril by Ann Prentice Wagner at Baltimore, Maryland. Interview by Ann Prentice Wagner. In person interview, May 20, 2013.

———. Interview with David Maril by Ann Prentice Wagner at Provincetown, Massachusetts. Interview by Ann Prentice Wagner. In person interview, July 27, 2010.

———. Interview with David Maril by Ann Prentice Wagner, Baltimore, Maryland. Interview by Ann Prentice Wagner. Oral interview, March 15, 2010.

———. Interview with David Maril by Ann Prentice Wagner, March 31, 2010. Interview by Ann Prentice Wagner, March 31, 2010.

———. "Re: Genealogy Research," October 4, 2015.

———. Telephone interview with David Maril by Ann Prentice Wagner. Interview by Ann Prentice Wagner. Telephone interview, May 20, 2016.

———."View Points by David Maril." Accessed August 6, 2015. http://www.hermanmaril.com/Herman_Maril_Paintings/View_Points.html.

Maril, Esta. Business. "Letter from Esta Maril to Bella Fishko." Business, November 26, 1984. Herman Maril Foundation.

———. "The Two Worlds of Herman Maril." In *Herman Maril: An Artist's Two Worlds.* Provincetown, Massachusetts: The Provincetown Art Association and Museum, 2008.

Maril, Herman. "A Green and Quiet Place to Live . . ." *The Baltimore Sun.* July 3, 1977, sec. K.

———. "Baltimore." Typescript. Baltimore, MD, undated. Herman Maril Foundation.

———.. "Herman Maril Journal," 1983 1971. Herman Maril Foundation.

———. Business. "Letter from Herman Maril to Edward B. Rowan Asking to Be Assigned to Overseas Unit." Business, June 13, 1943. Herman Maril Foundation.

———. Business. "Letter from Herman Maril to Elmira Bier of the Phillips Memorial Gallery about Purchases of Art by Duncan Phillips." Business, December 11, 1934. Phillips Collection.

———. Letter. "Letter from Herman Maril to Etta Cone about the Exhibition of Her Collection at the Baltimore Museum." Letter, June 7, 1941. Baltimore Museum of Art Archives, Cone Sisters Papers.

———.. Business. "Letter from Herman Maril to Forbes Watson." Business, April 12, 1934. Archives of American Art, Washington, D.C.

———. Business. "Letter from Herman Maril to George Levitine of the University of Maryland Requesting Sabbatical Leave." Business, April 1, 1968. Herman Maril Foundation.

———. Business. "Letter from Herman Maril to George Levitine of University of Maryland Requesting a Sabbatical." Business, January 16, 1975. Herman Maril Foundation.

———. Personal letter. "Letter from Herman Maril to His Cousin Maril B. Jacobs, October 18, 1980." Personal letter, October 18, 1980.

———. Personal letter. "Letter from Herman Maril to His Friend Selma Oppenheimer about His Military Service." Personal letter, December 8, 1943. Herman Maril Foundation.

———. Business. "Letter from Herman Maril to Richard Castellane." Business, December 11, 1962. Herman Maril Foundation.

———. Business. "Letter to George Levitine about Tapestries." Business, January 16, 1975.

———. Oral History Interview with Herman Maril by Dorothy Seckler for Archives of American Art, Provincetown, Massachusetts. Interview by Dorothy Seckler. Tape-recorded interview and transcript, July 5, 1965. Archives of American Art. http://www.aaa.si.edu/collections/interviews/oral-history-interview-herman-maril-11701.

———. Oral history interview with Herman Maril by Robert Brown for the Archives of American Art. Interview by Robert Brown. Sound Recording Transcript, July 21, 1971. Archives of American Art.

———. Oral History Interview with Herman Maril by Ronald Becker, Archives of American Art. Interview by Ronald Becker. Tape-recorded interview and transcript, July 22, 1981. Herman Maril Foundation.

———. "Places of Interest Free to Servicemen in Washington." *Baker's Batter,* May 1, 1944. Herman Maril Foundation.

———."Speech for University College Commencement." Typescript. Herman Maril Foundation, Baltimore, Maryland, 1985. Herman Maril Foundation.

———. "Supplemental Statement by Herman Maril about His Military Service and Ideas for Future Art Works," September 1944. Herman Maril Foundation.

———. "The WPA Art Project." *Baltimore Evening Sun*. June 25, 1943.

Maril, Herman, and William Bronk. *Painter & Poet: The Art of Herman Maril the Poems of William Bronk: A Collection of Letters*. Edited by Sheldon Hurst. Queensbury, New York: Adirondack Community College, 2008.

Maril, Herman., Christine M. McCarthy, Esta. Maril, Provincetown Art Association & Museum., Inc. David Findlay Jr., and Md.) Walters Art Gallery (Baltimore. *Herman Maril: An Artist's Two Worlds*. Provincetown, MA: Provincetown Art Association and Museum, 2008.

Maril, Nadja. Interview at Nadja Maril's house in Annapolis, Maryland. Interview by Ann Prentice Wagner. In person interview, June 19, 2011.

Maril, Nadja, and Herman Maril. *Me, Molly Midnight, the Artist's Cat*. Owings Mills, Md.: Stemmer House Publishers, 1977.

———. *Runaway Molly Midnight, the Artist's Cat*. Owings Mills, Md.: Stemmer House Publishers, 1980.

"Maril, Carnelli Painting on Exhibit in Baltimore." *Washington Post*. September 29, 1946, sec. S.

"Maril Exhibit Opens in N. Y." *Baltimore Sun*. March 31, 1974, sec. D.

"Maril in House Exh. List," undated. The Phillips Collection.

"Maril's Painting at Chicago Show." *Baltimore Sun*. October 31, 1943, sec. M.

Marling, Karal Ann. *Wall-to-Wall America: A Cultural History of Post-Office Murals in the Great Depression*. Minneapolis, Minnesota: University of Minnesota Press, 1982.

"Maryland Artists Recognized in Fair." *Baltimore Sun*. January 8, 1939.

"Maryland Institute Head Is Named by Governors." *The Baltimore Sun*. July 14, 1920.

"Maryland Institute Instructor Exhibits at Modernist Gallery." *The Baltimore Sun*. January 16, 1926.

"Maryland Soldier Wins Art Award at Baker General." *Washington Post*, March 26, 1945.

McGlauflin, Alice Coe. *Who's Who in American Art: Charles H. Walther*. Vol. 1. Washington, D.C.: The American Federation of Arts, 1935.

———. *Who's Who in American Art: Herman Maril*. Vol. 1. Washington, D.C.: The American Federation of Arts, 1935.

———., ed. *Who's Who in American Art: Herman Maril*. Vol. 2. Washington, D.C.: The American Federation of Arts, 1937.

McKinzie, Richard D. *The New Deal for Artists*. [Princeton: Princeton University Press, 1973.

Metropolitan Museum of Art. Business. "Letter from the Metropolitan Museum of Art to Herman Maril Saying That Press Release Would Soon Be Going out Announcing the Purchase of Paintings Including Maril's in the Kitchen." Business, August 1, 1940. Herman Maril Foundation.

———. *On the Bright Side: A Loan Exhibition of Contemporary American Painting & Sculpture*. New York, New York: Metropolitan Museum of Art, 1942.

Milch, Margot W., and Arnold L. Lehman. "Herman Maril." *Baltimore Sun*. September 20, 1986, sec. A.

Mocsanyi, Paul. *Karl Knaths*. Washington, D.C.: H.K. Press, 1957.

"Modern Artists' Group Finds Schuler 'Independent' Also." *Baltimore Sun*. February 4, 1929.

"Modernists' Art Class to Be Started Wednesday." *The Baltimore Sun*. January 13, 1928.

"Mr. Walther." *The Baltimore Sun*. July 31, 1929.

"Museum Aide to Talk on Progress in Art." *Baltimore Sun*. January 8, 1939, sec. SO.

Museum of Modern Art. *Painting and Sculpture from 16 American Cities*. New York: The Museum of Modern Art, 1933.

"Museum Will Show Baltimore Modernist Art for First Time." *The Baltimore Sun*. March 17, 1926.

Myers, Bernard S. *Modern Art in the Making*. New York: McGraw-Hill Book Company, Inc., 1959.

National Gallery of Art. "Invitation to Exhibition Preview for The American Artist and Water Reclamation, National Gallery of Art." National Gallery of Art, 1972.

National Society of Independent Artists. *Catalogue of the Second Exhibition 1933 of the National Society of Independent Artists*. Washington, D.C.: National Society of Independent Artists, 1933.

"N. Y. Gallery Sets Maril Art Exhibit." *Baltimore Evening Sun*. January 27, 1961.

Newman, Louis. "Cross Currents." In *Cross Currents: Milton Avery, Karl Knaths, Herman Maril*, 2. New York, New York: David Findlay Jr. Fine Art, 2007.

O'Brian, John. *Ruthless Hedonism: The American Reception of Matisse*. Chicago and London: The University of Chicago Press, 1999.

O'Connor, Francis V., ed. *WPA: Art for the Millions*. Greenwich, Connecticut: New York Graphic Society Ltd., 1973.

"Olin Dows, Artist Known for His Murals, Dies at 76." *New York Times*. June 7, 1981. http://www.nytimes.com/1981/obituaries/oilin-dows, artist known for his murals, dies at 76 · NYTimes.com.

"One-Man Exhibition." *Baltimore Sun*. August 22, 1968, sec. B.

Oppenheimer, Beverly. "Ex Parte in the Matter of the Petition of Hyman Becker for Change of Name." Circuit Court of Baltimore City, September 25, 1940. Maryland State Archives, Annapolis, Maryland.

Pagano, Grace. *Contemporary American Painting*. New York: Duell, Sloan and Pearce, 1945.

"Painting Selected for National Tour." *Baker's Batter: Newton D. Baker General Hospital*, November 15, 1944.

"Paintings Chosen for White House." *Washington Star*. May 12, 1934.

"Paintings from Phillips Gallery Will Be Shown." *The Baltimore Sun*. April 8, 1927.

Peoples, J. C. "Contact between The United States of America and Herman Maril, Artist," May 12, 1939. Herman Maril Foundation.

Perlman, Bennard B. *Herman Maril: Inaugural Exhibition, Baltimore Junior College*. Baltimore, Maryland: Baltimore Junior College, 1965.

Phillips, Duncan. *An Exhibition of Expressionist Painters from the Experiment Station of the Phillips Memorial Gallery*. Washington, D.C.: Phillips Memorial Gallery, 1927.

———. *Catalogue of the Exhibition of American Themes by American Painters Lent by Phillips Memorial Gallery, Washington, D.C.* Washington, D.C.: Phillips Memorial Gallery, 1927.

———. Business. "Letter from Duncan Phillips to Herman Maril Agreeing to Lend Gouache Old Mill to Exhibition at Howard University." Business, November 12, 1934. Herman Maril Foundation.

Phillips, Duncan, Erika D. Passantino, and David W. Scott. *The Eye of Duncan Phillips: A Collection in the Making*. Washington, DC: Phillips Collection in association with Yale University New Haven, 1999.

Phillips, Marjorie, and Phillips Collection. *Duncan Phillips and His Collection*. New York; London: W.W. Norton in association with the Phillips Collection, Washington, D.C., 1982.

Phillips Collection. *The Phillips Collection: A Summary Catalogue*. Washington, D.C.: The Collection, 1985.

Phillips Collection., and Eliza E. Rathbone. *Duncan Phillips Centennial Exhibition*. Washington, D.C.: Phillips Collection, 1999.

Pietila, Antero. *Not in My Neighborhood: How Bigotry Shaped a Great American City*. Chicago: Ivan R. Dee, 2010.

"'Pleased . . . by the Forms of Nature': Maril Exhibition to Honor Dr. Lord." *Baltimore Sun*. September 9, 1967, sec. A.

Portner, Leslie Judd. "Bader Opens a New Gallery." *Washington Post*. April 4, 1954, sec. ST.

"Public Occurrences." *Washington Post*. February 17, 1977, sec. MD.

Public Works of Art Project. "Class A Artist, Becker, Hermand [Sic] M., 3810 Park Heights Ave., Baltimore, MD," May 26, 1934. Baltimore Museum of Art Archives, Public Works of Art Project, Records for the State of Maryland.

———. "List of Heads of the 16 Regions, Public Works of Art Project, No. 1," Not dated. Baltimore Museum of Art Archives, Public Works of Art Project, Records for the State of Maryland.

———. *National Exhibition of Art, by the Public Works of Art Project, April 24, 1934 to May 20, 1934 (Inclusive) the Corcoran Gallery of Art, Washington, District of Columbia*. Washington, D.C.: U. S. Government Printing Office, 1934.

———. "Public Works of Art Project Pay Roll," May 27, 1934. Baltimore Museum of Art Archives, Public Works of Art Project, Records for the State of Maryland.

———. "Region - 4, Committee Personnel," January 30, 1034. Baltimore Museum of Art Archives, Public Works of Art Project, Records for the State of Maryland.

"PWAP Art Show Here: Exhibition to Be Opened at Modern Museum Wednesday." *New York Times*. September 16, 1934, sec. N.

Rasmussen, Fred. "Monumental City's Monument Maker Sculptor: Hans Schuler Left His Mark on the Maryland Institute, College of Art and in Many Public Places around His Hometown." *The Baltimore Sun*. October 19, 1997.

"Region 4 List of Projects," 1934. Baltimore Museum of Art Archives, Public Works of Art Project, Records for the State of Maryland.

"Regional Show Winners." *Baltimore Sun*. March 10, 1963, sec. A.

Rehert, Isaac. "The Need to Give Oneself More Time." *The Baltimore Sun*. February 28, 1977, sec. B.

Renninger, Christian. "Herman Maril: Hanging around Admiralty House." *Precis*, November 7, 1975.

Rewald, John, and Frances Weitzenhoffer. *Cézanne and America: Dealers, Collectors, Artists and Critics 1891-1921*. Princeton, N.J.: Princeton University Press, 1989.

Richard, Paul. "Paintings at the Corcoran Cause Hostility by Viewers." *Washington Post*. March 31, 1968, sec. G.

Richardson, Brenda., William C. Ameringer, and Baltimore Museum of Art. *Dr Claribel & Miss Etta: The Cone Collection of the Baltimore Museum of Art*. [Baltimore, Md.]: [Baltimore Museum of Art], 1985.

Rishel, Joseph J., Katherine. Sachs, Roberta. Bernstein, Paul Cézanne, and Philadelphia Museum of Art. *Cézanne and beyond*. Philadelphia, PA; New Haven: Philadelphia Museum of Art; In Association with Yale University Press, 2009.

Robert Carlen Gallery. "Recent Paintings by Herman Maril." Robert Carlen Gallery, 1947.

Robinson, Roxana. *Georgia O'Keeffe: A Life*. Hanover and London: University Press of New England, 1989.

Rodda, Larry C. "Tells Dr. Boas How Little He Knows About the Modern Art Situation in Baltimore." *The Baltimore Sun*. November 12, 1926.

Rowan, Edward B. Business. "Letter from Edward B. Rowan to Herman Maril about Altavista, Virginia, Post Office Mural Two Inch Scale Color Sketch." Business, May 27, 1939. Herman Maril Foundation.

———. Business. "Letter from Edward B. Rowan to Herman Maril about West Scranton Branch Post Office Mural." Business, January 28, 1941. Herman Maril Foundation.

———. Business. "Letter from Edward B. Rowan to Herman Maril Commending His Art Seen at Studio House and Saying He Is Glad Maril Had Been Hired on to PWAP." Business, January 23, 1934. Herman Maril Foundation.

———. Business. "Letter from Edward B. Rowan to Herman Maril Saying His Sketch of Old Baltimore Water Front Had Arrived and Was Much Appreciated." Business, February 17, 1934. Herman Maril Foundation.

———. Business. "Letter from Edward B. Rowan to Herman Maril Saying His Work Has Won a Purchase Award in the O. E. M. Competition for Pictures to Record Defense and War Activities." Business, February 5, 1942. Herman Maril Foundation.

Rowles, Louise, and Bill Rowles. Interview at the Rowles' home in Baltimore. Interview by Ann Prentice Wagner. In person interview, April 27, 2010.

"Sale of Pictures Elates Independent Artists." *Baltimore Sun*. March 29, 1929.

Sawyer, Kenneth B. "A Place of Mystery and Beauty." *Baltimore Sun*. February 7, 1960, sec. A.

———. "Guggenheim, Baltimore Acquisitions." *Baltimore Sun*. July 14, 1957, sec. F.

———. *Herman Maril: Recent Paintings*. Cape Cod, Massachusetts: Wellfleet Art Gallery, 1964.

———. "Maril Exhibition in Capital." *Baltimore Sun*. April 30, 1961, sec. A.

———. "'Sad Shake of Head' over Art Festival." *Baltimore Sun*. August 17, 1958, sec. F.

Sawyer, Kenneth B. "Gala Events at Provincetown." *Baltimore Sun*. September 2, 1956.

Schoettler, Carl. "Herman Maril: The Confidence That Comes with Half a Century of Painting." *Baltimore Evening Sun*. March 1, 1983, sec. C.

Scott, David W. "The Evolution of a Critic: Changing Views in the Writings of Duncan Phillips." In *The Eye of Duncan Phillips: A Collection in the Making*, 9–22. Washington, D.C., New Haven and London: The Phillips Collection in association with Yale University Press, 1999.

Scott, William B., and Peter M. Rutkoff. *New York Modern: The Arts and the City*. Baltimore and London: The Johns Hopkins University Press, 1999.

Shen, Fern. "Storm Fells Four-Century-Old Baltimore Tree." *Baltimore Brew*. October 30, 2012. https://www.baltimorebrew.com/2012/10/30/storm-fells-four-century-old-baltimore-tree/.

Sherwin, Mark. Interview at Mark Sherwin's Studio, Provincetown, Massachusetts. Interview by Ann Prentice Wagner. In person interview, October 8, 2011.

"Slightly Different Dunes: But Local Artists Still out to Paint." *Provincetown Advocate*. December 4, 1969.

Soldier Art. Fighting Forces Series. Infantry Journal, 1945.

Solender, Elsa A. "Baltimore Painter Herman Maril: Silent Serenity and Complex Logic." *Baltimore Jewish Times*, March 15, 1985.

———. "Visions Rich & Simple: Painter Herman Maril Has Spent a Lifetime Paring down a Complex Vision to the Bare Essentials." *The Messenger*, April 11, 1984.

Sproul, Adelaide. *Cummington School of the Arts: A School of the Imagination*. Watertown, Massachusetts: Windflower Press, 1991.

Stevens, Elisabeth. "Retirement Lets Herman Maril Get It Together." *The Baltimore Sun*. April 6, 1980, sec. D.

"Studio House Artists Show in Philadelphia." *ARTnews (U.S.A.)*, February 8, 1936. The Phillips Collection.

"Summer Classes in Art Announced by U. of Md." *Baltimore Sun*. April 19, 1948.

"Summer News of Art." *New York Sun*. August 15, 1936.

Summerford, Ben L. "Part I: The Phillips Collection and Art in Washington." In *The Eye of Duncan Phillips: A Collection in the Making*, 607–35. Washington, D.C., New Haven and London: The Phillips Collection in association with Yale University Press, 1990.

Sweaney, B.W. "C. H. Walther Is Ousted by MD. Institute." *The Baltimore Sun*. July 30, 1929.

T., S. "Herman Maril." *Arts Magazine*, April 1962.

Taylor, Francis Henry. Business. "Letter from Francis Henry Taylor, Director of Metropolitan Museum of Art, to Herman Maril about His Art's Being One of the Works Available to the Museum's Extension Service." Business, July 12, 1940. Herman Maril Foundation.

The Cummington School, Cummington, Massachusetts, 1937. Cummington, Massachusetts: Playhouse-in-the-Hills, 1937.

"The Legacy of the Schuler School of Fine Arts." Education. *Schuler School of Fine Arts*, 2014. http://www.schulerschool.com/legacy.php.

The Whyte Gallery. *Paintings by Herman Maril*. Washington, D.C.: The Whyte Gallery, 1940.

———. "Young Washington Paintings: Former 'Studio House' Exhibitors." The Whyte Gallery, 1939.

Thoreau, Henry David. *Cape Cod*. New York: Penguin Group, 1987.

Treasury Department, Public Works of Art Project. "Class A Artist Herman M. Becker." Treasury Department, Public Works of Art Project, May 26, 1934. Baltimore Museum of Art Archives, Public Works of Art Project, Records for the State of Maryland.

"Two Teachers Added at University." *Baltimore Sun*. September 16, 1946.

University of Maryland, College Park, and University of Maryland, College Park. *350 Years of Art & Architecture in Maryland*. Edited by Mary A. Dean and Arthur R. Blumenthal. College Park: Art Gallery, and Gallery of the School of Architecture, University of Maryland, 1984.

University of Maryland, University College. "Herman Maril Honorary Degree of Doctor of Fine Arts, University of Maryland, University College, January 5, 1985." University of Maryland, University College, January 5, 1985. The Phillips Collection.

University of Maryland University College. *His Own Path: The Spirit and Legacy of Herman Maril*. College Park, Maryland: University of Maryland University College, 2011.

Van Hook, Katrina. "Gouaches Are Put on Display Here." *Washington Post*. December 2, 1945, sec. B.

Vaughan, Malcolm. "Modern Museum Exhibits Art Produced by New Deal." *New York American*. September 1934.

"View Points by David Maril." Accessed August 6, 2015. http://www.herman-maril.com/Herman_Maril_Paintings/View_Points.html.

Vikan, Gary. "Forward." In *Herman Maril: An Artist's Two Worlds*. Provincetown, Massachusetts: The Provincetown Art Association and Museum, 2008.

Wagner, Ann. "'Living On Paper:' Georgia O'Keeffe and the Culture of Drawing and Watercolor in the Stieglitz Circle." University of Maryland, 2005.

Wagner, Ann Prentice. *1934: A New Deal for Artists*. Washington, D.C.: Smithsonian American Art Museum, 2009.

Walker, Hudson D. Business. "From Hudson D. Walker to Herman Maril Telling Him Two of His Works Are on Approval at the Metropolitan Museum of Art." Business, April 30, 1940. Herman Maril Foundation.

Walston, Mark. *Historic Photos of Baltimore*. Baltimore, Maryland: Turner Publishing Company, 2008.

Walther, Charles. Business. "Letter from Charles H. Walther to R. J. McKinney Asking to Be Placed on PWAP Rolls." Business, December 13, 1933. Baltimore Museum of Art Archives, Public Works of Art Project, Records for the State of Maryland.

"Walther to Head Club Art School." *The Baltimore Sun*. September 29, 1930.

Watrous, James. *American Printmaking: A Century of American Printmaking, 1880-1980*. Madison, Wisc.: Univ. of Wisconsin Press, 1984.

Watson, Forbes. "A Steady Job." *The American Magazine of Art*, April 1934.

"WCFM to Carry Music Festival." *Washington Post*. April 1, 1951, sec. L.

Wellfleet Art Gallery. "Invitation to Exhibition of Herman Maril Paintings, Abbott Pattison Sculpture, Wellfleet Art Gallery, July 29, - August 10, 1974." Wellfleet Art Gallery, 1974.

Wharton, Carol. "A union that doesn't advocate shorter hours." *Baltimore Sun*. November 18, 1951, sec. MM.

Wheeler, Tim. "Storm Claims Baltimore's Oldest, Largest Tree." *Baltimore Sun*. October 31, 2012. http://articles.baltimoresun.com/2012-10-31/features/bal-bmg-storm-claims-one-of-baltimores-oldest-largest-trees-20121031_1_tree-species-druid-hill-park-city-forestry-workers.

White, Michelle. "Going Blind: Drawings in the 1970s." In *Master Drawings*, 4th ed. Vol. 52. New York: Master Drawings Association, Inc., 2014.

Whyte Gallery. "New Paintings by Herman Maril." Whyte Gallery, 1944.

"Whyte Show Opens March 20." *Washington Post*. March 15, 1938.

Wiener, Philip P. "In Memoriam: George Boas (1891-1980)." *Journal of the History of Ideas* 41, no. 3 (September 1980): 453–56.

"Will Discuss Modernism." *The Baltimore Sun*. January 21, 1926.

"Will Not Oppose Instructor's Exhibiting of Modernist Work." *The Baltimore Sun*. January 17, 1926.

Wilson, Vylla Poe. "Lithographs of Daumier, 19th Century French Painter-Caricaturist, Shown at Public Library." *Washington Post*. December 2, 1934, sec. SO.

Wilson, Vylla Poe. "Fourteenth Biennial Exhibition Focuses Art World's Eyes on Corcoran Gallery Here." *Washington Post*. March 3, 1935, sec. SA.

Wooden, Howard E. "Herman Maril: A Retrospective Exhibition of Paintings, 1926-1983." Wichita Art Museum, March 26, 1984.

"Works of Local Artists to Be Shown at Chicago." *Baltimore Sun*. October 14, 1938.

Yount, Sylvia, and Elizabeth Johns. *To Be Modern: American Encounters with Cezanne and Company*. Pennsylvania: University of Pennsylvania Press, 1996.

Fig. 11. Herman and Esta Maril in their Baltimore Home in 1968, Herman Maril Foundation